THE 21 IRREFUTABLE TRUTHS OF TRADING

A Trader's Guide to
Developing a Mind to Win

John H. Hayden

McGraw-Hill

New York   San Francisco   Washington, D.C.   Auckland   Bogotá
Caracas   Lisbon   London   Madrid   Mexico City   Milan
Montreal   New Delhi   San Juan   Singapore
Sydney   Tokyo   Toronto

Library of Congress Cataloging-in-Publication Data

Hayden, John H.
   The 21 irrefutable truths of trading : a trader's guide to developing a mind to win / by John H. Hayden.
      p.   cm.
   ISBN 0-07-135789-0
   1. Stocks.   I. Title: Twenty-one irrefutable truths of trading : a trader's guide to developing a mind to win.   II. Title: Trader's guide to developing a mind to win.   III. Title.
HG4661.H39   2000
332.63'22—dc21

99-057176
CIP

McGraw-Hill

A Division of The McGraw·Hill Companies

1 2 3 4 5 6 7 8 9 0   DOC/DOC   0 9 8 7 6 5 4 3 2 1 0

ISBN 0-07-135789-0

This book was set in Times New Roman by Kim Sheran and Paul Scozzari of McGraw-Hill's Professional Book Group composition unit, Hightstown, N.J.

Printed and bound by R. R. Donnelley & Sons Company.

This publication is designed to provide accurate and authoritative information in regard to the subject matter covered. It is sold with the understanding that neither the author nor the publisher is engaged in rendering legal, accounting, or other professional service. If legal advice or other expert assistance is required, the services of a competent professional person should be sought.

> *—From a Declaration of Principles jointly adopted by a Committee of the American Bar Association and a Committee of Publishers.*

McGraw-Hill books are available at special quantity discounts to use as premiums and sales promotions, or for use in corporate training programs. For more information, please write to the Director of Special Sales, Professional Publishing, McGraw-Hill, Two Penn Plaza, New York, NY 10121-2298. Or contact your local bookstore.

 This book is printed on recycled, acid-free paper containing a minimum of 50% recycled, de-inked fiber.

To my three children,
Allison, Christopher, and Melissa,
who are truly a gift from God.

Contents

v

Part 2. The Strategies of Successful Trading

Acknowledgments

I AM DEEPLY GRATEFUL to everyone who has helped me in the preparation of this manuscript. Thank you to Christopher Castroviejo CTA, Mary Lemmons Ph.D., Frank Hayden, Joseph Hayden, Toni Leo Ph.D., and Tom Manglis. I am also very grateful to all the individuals who have taken the time to teach me many of the concepts that are in this book. Thank you to Andrew Cardwell Jr. CTA, Anthony Robbins, Dr. Richard McCall, and Michael Clarke CTA.

Without a doubt this book would not have been possible without the understanding, patience, and support of Allison and Christopher Hayden, my two children who still live with me.

In addition, I am grateful to my editor Stephen Isaacs, who had the gift to see the promise in a very rough manuscript. I would also like to thank the following individuals for their support and encouragement: Carol Dannenhauer, Todd Fulton, Albert Harkins, Robert Koehler, Peter Koehler, John Proctor, Jermy Lawson, and Jack Karczewski.

John H. Hayden

The Virtues, Vices, and Beliefs of Outstanding Traders

1

INTRODUCTION

Not in the clamor of the crowded street,
Nor in the shouts and plaudits of the throng,
But in ourselves lie triumph and defeat.

—HENRY WADSWORTH LONGFELLOW

I don't like money, actually...but it helps calm my nerves.

—JOE LOUIS

During my 87 years I have witnessed a whole succession
of technological revolutions. But none of them has done
away with the need for character in the individual, or the
ability to think.

—BERNARD BARUCH

EVERY YEAR THOUSANDS of very successful individuals make a decision to start investing in stocks, or trading: commodities, currencies, or stocks. All traders are on a constant quest for knowledge that will help them increase their profitability. Most individuals decide to start investing or trading for a variety of logical and emotional reasons, many of which have not been adequately addressed. The goal of this book is to help you make your quest easier and less painful. Let me begin by asking you a key question: What do you really want to accomplish as a trader or investor? The market will give you incredible pleasure if you approach it correctly. However, if you approach trading and the market from the wrong direction, you'll receive incredible pain!

There are two primary ingredients for success in any endeavor: mastery of your physical environment, and mastery of your internal mental environment. When it comes to markets, the physical environment consists of numbers— namely, prices. The cold, hard truth is that prices can do absolutely anything tomorrow—it is impossible to predict with certainty where they will be. The best you can do is determine what prices will probably occur tomorrow. To do so, you need to have a trading methodology that gives you an edge.

Unfortunately, before you can ever hope to truly have an edge, you must first master your internal environment. Your internal environment consists of your beliefs, values, and rules. It is how you perceive the external market. Think about the times you achieved a new goal in the past. After achieving it, were you the same person you were when you initially started? Have you thought about what type of person you must become to be a successful trader or investor?

This book is intended to give you as many advantages as possible to help you dramatically increase the amount of your profits and speed at which you generate them. While the language in this book is geared toward traders in the commodity, currency, and derivative markets, the information is just as valid for long-term stock investors.

As a group, new traders consist largely of very successful people. Doctors, attorneys, airline pilots, and entrepreneurs comprise the four largest groups who decide every year to try their hand at trading. Of course, outside of these four primary groups new commodity traders have a vast and varied background. This categorization is less true for stock traders.

Traders have lost billions of dollars in the pursuit of profits. They have spent millions of dollars to purchase computer trading programs, attend seminars, and read trading books. *Sadly, the average new trader will lose most if not all of his or her trading capital within four to eight months of opening a trading account.*

The fact that a constant supply of new individuals decides to start trading is evident by the low renewal rate for the two major trading magazines in the United States. It is also obvious by the same ads being run in these magazines consistently targeting new traders. You can open any financial newspaper to find a plethora of ads that target new traders. Then there is the educational trading seminar industry, which generates millions of dollars every year: the more popular seminars targeting the new trader are always sold out.

The allure of trading is indeed very powerful. Where else can an individual investor turn $10,000 into $1 million within a year? Where else can an individual earn a 500 percent return? Everywhere new traders turn they see or hear about the fabulous returns earned by some traders. Every new trader can tell you how George Soros made over $1 billion within a few days when the British pound depreciated. Every new trader wants a piece of that action.

After all, everyone will tell the new trader that statistically 90 percent of all traders lose their trading capital within 12 months, *but* 10 percent increase their capital. The implication, to the beginning trader, is that 10 percent of the traders are wildly successful. Most new traders never suspect that the assumptions they are making from this statistic are flawed. Since most individuals who become new traders are already in the upper 10 percent of their chosen profession, they naturally assume that they will get into that upper 10 percent of successful traders. The fly in the ointment is that the 9-to-1 (lose-to-succeed) ratio often bandied about is based on the total universe of traders trading in a 12-month period. *It is a ratio based not on new traders, but on all traders.* The unfortunate truth is that it takes 100 new traders to produce one or two new traders who are net profitable after 12 months. The average life expectancy of a new trader before losing 65 to 95 percent of the money they opened their account with is four to six months!

When an individual makes the decision to start trading commodities, he or she is faced with a multitude of choices, similar to when the individual started his or her professional career. The huge difference is that most people build their professional careers in a structured learning environment—typically in a university or business setting. Almost without exception they enter that "10 percent winners' circle" in their respective careers *slowly.* In trading there is no structured learning environment, there are no professors or business clients to guide the trader in how to think, behave, and trade. Most beginning traders will attend a seminar or two, read a few books, buy a computer-based trading program, and get a data feed. They then open a trading account with $5000 to $20,000, fully expecting to earn triple-digit returns.

Inherent in new traders' decisions is the belief that trading is easy once they possess the "holy grail." As their accounts start to change either up or down, the traders will start to form psychological opinions that ultimately cause their demise and loss of trading funds. This happens whether the trader is initially profitable or starts losing from the very beginning.

The trader's success is ultimately determined by his or her psychological perceptions and beliefs. Most if not all new traders really believe that there *is* a "holy grail"—in the form of a *computer-based trading program* that all successful traders use with some minor variations. New traders are convinced that if they have the same computer trading program, the same sources of information, and the same data feed as a "trading wizard," they too will be wildly successful. Most new traders believe that success in trading can be bought by installing a trading program or reading a few technical books.

In their work lives, if these new traders were asked whether reading a book could lead to professional success, they would have a hearty laugh! Whether they are doctors, business owners, or service professionals, they all know that the only way to become a success is through years of commitment. Why, then, do most new traders think the learning process can be short-circuited?

Most new traders honestly believe that they can take the same skills they developed to get to the top in their chosen profession and apply them to trading. These skills are typically hard work, study, persistence, and experience.

How do you as a new trader avoid making some of these mistakes in the first place? The easy answer is to realize that your trading success will be ultimately determined by your psychological perceptions, beliefs, and attitudes. The trading game is played out in the six inches of space between your ears! Just as in golf! You need to make sure the beliefs that you develop about trading are based on logical and correct assumptions.

In any profession, from doctor to football player, there are certain truths that dramatically increase the speed of success. A football player lifts weights and physically pushes his body to its limits so that he can be a strong performer. However, a physically powerful football player is worthless if he lacks a valid strategy and, as you will see, certain key beliefs and values. Similarly, a trader must expand his or her knowledge of trading strategies and must also possess certain key beliefs and values.

There are certain universal truths about trading that all successful traders hold dear to their hearts. These universal truths constitute the actual "holy grail." Once discovered, the truths are self-evident, yet they are very hard to unearth without a lot of hard work.

What are these universal truths? And why until now has no one mentioned them in a seminar or publication? The universal laws of trading are the virtues, vices, and strategies described in this book.

Who am I to state that there is a holy grail that everyone else has overlooked? How can I say that there are certain fundamental, irrefutable truths of trading? After all, many sophisticated traders have written books and taught a wide variety of trading methodologies. Why have they all missed what is so obvious?

The answer is straightforward. As far as I can tell, no one is willing to publicly admit that there are certain immutable truths about trading. These truths consist of certain internal beliefs and values that demand work and time to develop. They cannot be bought today, studied tonight, and applied tomorrow in the next trading session.

Immutable truths apply in every arena of life. In nature, fish cannot fly, and eagles cannot swim, yet both require oxygen to live. Skyscrapers must be built from steel and concrete, not wood, and must rise from a solid foundation. Rockets can escape to space only by obeying the laws of physics. So it follows that there are certain immutable trading truths that all successful traders adhere to.

Most new traders believe that success is achievable if they have enough money, determination, or creativity. Human nature wants to believe that anything is possible. New traders want to believe that they belong in the 10 percent winners' circle, and that they will enter that circle quickly and easily. Human nature also wants to believe that these immutable truths of trading are easy to set in motion, that they are mechanical, and that a computer can implement them.

If new traders stay at trading long enough, they will slowly start to accept that there are certain truths that must at all costs be obeyed. Once a trader accepts this fact, a lot of the stress, uncertainty, and frustration leaves. The challenge is that most new traders never get to that point. They quit before ever discovering that they lost their money because they were violating some if not all of the irrefutable truths. Once they open their minds to the truths in trading, it's easy for traders to see what they are.

I started trading stocks in 1976, physical gold in 1982, and U.S. Treasury bonds in 1993. Trading has been an obsession of mine for more than two decades. What I have found is that all outstanding traders—be it in commodities, stocks, diamonds, or horses—have accepted certain immutable facts about what and how they trade! There are certain virtues that they have all worked to strengthen, and certain vices they have labored to annihilate.

After years of being obsessed about what makes a great trader, I can tell you unequivocally that all great traders obey the "natural laws" of trading. None of these truths has anything to do with the methodology traders use, what markets they trade, or how they trade. None of the truths can be programmed into a computer; however, they can be programmed into the mind.

Every individual who has become truly excellent in a chosen profession or career has done so by increasing desirable personality characteristics and decreasing or getting rid of less desirable characteristics.

Every individual who has become excellent in a chosen profession or career has done so by strengthening personal virtues and controlling vices. In today's world it may seem a little strange to talk about virtues and vices. Make no mistake. It is the same foundation that all successful individuals use to excel in their professional careers.

This book is my attempt to help shorten the amount of time it takes a trader to become profitable. It is my way of returning to the market some of the joy, passion, and fulfillment that I have obtained by being a trader.

> Every trader has strengths and weaknesses. As long as you stick to your own style, you get the good and the bad in your own approach. When you try to incorporate someone else's style, you often wind up with the worst of both styles. I've done that a lot.
>
> —Michael Marcus

New traders believe that all it takes to succeed in trading is a "holy grail" trading system. Nearly all beginners are convinced that the only thing separating them from unlimited wealth is a trading system that the "professionals" use. If they could only have tomorrow's *Wall Street Journal* today, they would be rich. Barring that, most new traders would gladly sell their birthright if they could have the computer trading program used by any of the "professional" stock or commodity trading wizards.

After all, wouldn't you love to have the same computer trading program as George Soros or Warren Buffett? Without hesitation, new traders go out and buy the newest, fastest, super-duper computer available. They then spend a great deal of effort deciding what computer trading program to purchase. In reality, there are only two types of programs available: a black box that tells you to buy the S&P Index at a certain price, or a program that allows you to write your own program to analyze the market.

Some new traders also attend seminars to learn the latest trading technique or system. Other traders decide that they don't want to work with a computer and its related programs, and instead look to a particular newsletter, fax, or e-mail, for the inside scoop. So they decide to take the trades recommended to them.

Keep in mind that the vast majority of traders (new and old) are very intelligent, and have achieved a high degree of success in their chosen professions. Because of the frantic rush not to miss the next huge move in corn futures, or the next Microsoft, most traders never stop to question the underlying premise that all of this activity is based on.

The fact that there are traders (in stocks, commodities, and currencies) who consistently remain profitable over time is undeniable. The fact that they earn huge sums of money is equally well known. It is also true that most (but not all) traders use computer programs to crunch the data, and that these computer programs are considered top secret.

These facts lead just about everyone to assume that top traders are successful because they have a program to correctly analyze and predict the market action. Everyone is focusing on the computer power, the computer program, and the quality of the data feed or news that these successful traders possess. No one is asking what came first: the individual's ability as a trader or the program?

The holy grail cannot be bought! Insofar as most traders are concerned, it does not really exist. Allow me to put this perception to rest at last—to toss it in a casket and tightly nail the lid shut. Suppose by some miracle you woke up and discovered that the great trader's fairy in the sky had installed the same trading program as used by Paul Tudor Jones in your computer, while you were sleeping. Even so, you *would never, ever make the same type of return as P. T. Jones!*

There is no newsletter, fax, or e-mail service that will make you millions. There is no computer program that will open secret doors. Forget about the overnight e-mail advisory line or the Internet chat room. Neither will make you rich. Forget it!

I am sorry to burst a bubble cherished by so many novice traders. After talking to hundreds of traders, and reviewing thousands of accounts, I can tell you that there simply isn't a holy grail *as perceived by the novice trader.*

Let me ask you several questions.

1. For a few thousand dollars you can buy many programs that promise to reliably make you several hundred percent. Why, then, is such a program for sale? Why doesn't the programmer start a hedge fund or become a commodity trading adviser (CTA) and earn many millions more?

2. Why doesn't a newsletter service allow you to see its past recommendations?

3. Why is it that most newsletter writers offer only generic-type entries? For example, they say that support for gold is at 300. They don't say buy gold at 300.5 and place a sell stop at 270.5. Why is that?

4. Why is it that the best hedge funds, mutual funds, commodity traders, and CTAs all use different trading methodologies?

5. Why was it possible for Bernard Baruch to amass millions (and keep them) back when the word "computer" didn't even exist?

6. Why is it that everyone seems to talk about Jessie Livermore as one of the great all-time traders, when in reality he committed suicide and was dead broke? (This last question is a pet peeve of mine; however, it is important.)

Sorry, folks. There is no easy way to make millions from thousands, without a lot of very hard work. As P. T. Barnum said, "There is a sucker born every minute." Substitute loser and you have the trading scene pretty accurately portrayed.

About now you are probably saying, "Well, wait a minute. What about that 10 percent of traders who make it?" Good question; let me address it. It seems that just about everyone recites the statistic that 90 percent of all traders lose, and 10 percent win. Just about all novice traders hear this and think, "Well, if 90 percent of all traders lose, then 10 percent win all the money the other 90 percent lost. Since I am smarter than most, I too will get into that 10 percent winners' circle, and get rich."

Implied in this reasoning is that 90 percent of all *new* traders lose, and 10 percent of all *new* traders win. Again I have to get my trusty pin out, and pop yet another bubble. The statistical 90 percent is on *all* traders in a year. Hence 10 percent of *all* traders make money. Now let us think for a second. Only 10 percent of all traders make money, and more experience is likely to improve their chances of success. By definition, a novice trader is inexperienced. Therefore, far more than 90 percent of new traders must lose their trading funds.

In a three-month period (September to December 1998), I talked to more than 500 new traders (people whose accounts were less than a year old), and with three exceptions they all had lost, or were in the process of losing, their trading capital! The brokerage house I worked for on average opens 50 accounts a day, with $5000 being the minimum account size allowed. This equals $50 million in annual losses among individuals who as a group were smart and successful in their chosen professions!

As a group they either were following an advisory service or "black box" trading system or had attempted to write their own trading system on a technical analysis trading program. They were all losing money. I really hope I have your attention by now. Did you know that when you open an account at a large trading firm, the salesperson who sets up the account gets credit only for the amount of money you opened the account with? Furthermore, did you know that the salesperson can usually get credit only for the next 30 days for any additional funds deposited with the brokerage house? Can you guess why? Let me give you a hint. What do you suppose is the average length of time before an account is closed?

In order to maintain a new account, the average novice trader will need to add more money within 60 days. Most traders will stop trading within four to six months after opening the account. That is how long it takes them to lose their money. The real believers in a computer-based holy grail will stop trading, do some more research, buy another program, or switch newsletters, and then re-fund their account.

Are you starting to get the message that you cannot buy a holy grail trading system, be it computer or advisory based? Are you starting to wonder why you bought this book? This is good! There is some good news, but you must really understand that you cannot buy a way to make millions. There is no way to become a great trader without a lot of work.

My goal is to show you the way. I cannot make you a great trader; only you can do that. There is a holy grail and you already have it! It is inside you, and what is preventing you from getting there are your perceptions, beliefs, and a lot of promotional/advertising garbage that only confuses and perplexes you.

The holy grail is this: Great traders are great not because of some computer program they use but because they have the ability to control their reality. The computer provides the information; it does not supply the thinking.

"Information is not a substitute for thinking!"

Great traders understand how critically their profitability depends upon their ability to strengthen their virtues and annihilate their vices. Ask any great trader how important emotional control or discipline is to financial success. You will get a very similar response. A great trader today would have been a great trader in tulips 600 years ago and would excel at trading in asteroid minerals 1000 years hence. This is because even though the technological tools available to great traders may vary, their ability to master their own internal beliefs and values remains constant.

All great traders have grasped these truths, and without a doubt would gladly give up their computer trading programs rather than give up their mental perceptions, beliefs, or values. This is why you as a trader would not even come close to obtaining the same returns as Paul T. Jones using the same computer program. You do not have the same mental perceptions, beliefs, values, or rules as he does.

The truth about the holy grail is that it is impossible to purchase, that it is not something you can program into a computer, and that all great traders (living and dead) have (or had) possession of it. This is because they all had very similar beliefs about the importance of mastering their virtues and eliminating their vices. The holy grail is nothing other than the self-examined life lived according to 21 irrefutable truths.

2

EGOTISTICAL TRADERS AND TRADERS WITH FALSE BELIEFS ALWAYS LOSE

The main obstacle lies in distancing ourselves from our emotions.

—BERNARD BARUCH

Win or lose, everybody gets what they want out of the market. Some people seem to like to lose, so they win by losing.

—ED SEYKOTA

EGO IS CLASSICALLY defined as the conscious component of the psyche that experiences the outside world and reacts to it. In all cases the ego is a component of the trader's psyche that must be disciplined. Your ego is what creates your self-image.

Your ego is the part of your psyche that experiences and reacts to three demands: the demands of the outside world, unconscious desires and thoughts, and conscious thought. In many cases the conscious mind tends to act as a policeman toward the more hedonistic, impulsive unconscious mind, and our ego mediates between the two in line with the beliefs we have. As an individual you can never get rid of your ego in an absolute sense; however, you can master and control how effectively it mediates between rational and irrational thoughts.

In other words, when traders look at the market, they are perceiving the market action through "sunglasses" that color their perception. Traders create these "sunglasses" by their beliefs about themselves, their beliefs about the market, their thoughts about the meaning of everything they are experiencing, and their desires. In order to be consistently profitable, the trader must remove the sunglasses.

As a trader, your outside world consists of the market, which is uncontrollable. Your unconscious thoughts and desires are also uncontrollable, since they reside in your unconscious mind. However, your unconscious mind is totally unable to tell the difference between what has actually been experienced and what has been vividly imagined. Consequently your unconscious mind, though uncontrollable, can be powerfully influenced. This is an important concept to remember. The conscious mind gives you the ability to decide — to think rationally and logically. In other words, your unconscious mind will often generate impulsive irrational thoughts that could lead to impulsive behavior unless they come under the control of the conscious rational mind. By using our conscious mind to become aware of the impulsive/irrational aspects of our unconscious mind, and controlling the thoughts we focus on, we will be able to control our behavior.

Most of us describe an egotistical person as someone who is arrogant, vain, or self-centered. This is because a person with an "inflated ego" is not able to correctly balance the three demands: the outside world, the unconscious mind, and the conscious mind. Consequently the egotist is a self-important jerk who believes that he or she is the center of the universe with little regard for the needs, desires, and wants of others.

Traders who "have an ego" are unable to perceive the market action correctly; consequently they consistently lose money. The reason their perception of the outside world is incorrect is that the reality of the market is being overpowered by their unconscious and conscious thoughts. The primary responsibility of a trader is to maintain an unbiased perspective that leads to unemotional and nonimpulsive decisions. Egocentric traders allow their beliefs to influence the ability of the rational conscious mind to correctly perceive the market action. In almost all cases, the novice trader will allow the conscious mind to focus on very disempowering beliefs, values, and virtues, thereby influencing the unconscious mind to generate even more disempowering unconscious thoughts.

Your ego wants to see you as a successful trader, regardless of the action of the market. There isn't a trader around who doesn't want to be successful in his or her own eyes and in the eyes of friends, family members, and the professional community.

Without exception, every outstanding trader has managed through a lot of very hard work to get control of the thoughts that the conscious mind focuses on. To become an excellent trader, you must get to the point where you are able to perceive the market as it actually is—not as your conscious or unconscious mind thinks it should be! Your sense of self will try to fool you into believing that you are not egocentric. The truth of the matter is that an overblown ego is the biggest single threat to a trader's profitability.

Ask all the really successful athletes, scientists, traders, business leaders, or salespeople how important it was to their ultimate success to master their conscious mind and discipline their unconscious mind. Every single one will tell you that it was absolutely essential.

Mastery of the conscious and unconscious mind is something that you must diligently work at. There is no easy way to achieve it except by hard work and persistence. Regardless of your age or experience, an undisciplined mind will absolutely prevent you from perceiving the market as it is. When you are unable to see the market as it is, you will be unable to create profits. In fact there is a direct relationship between your ability to control your mind and your ability to generate trading profits.

An egotistical trader will often define "winning" within a very short-term time frame (in a very myopic way). In other words, the trader will insist that every trade must be a winner, or that a successful trader always ends the day or week in profit. Professional traders have a different perspective. Typically they adopt a more long-term outlook that incorporates a much longer series of trades. A longer-term perspective (allowing for more trades) allows professionals to deal with their beliefs about themselves and the market more effectively. Consequently each trade doesn't have to be profitable; in fact, losing trades are actually expected.

A surefire recipe for failure is for a trader to have an egotistical belief system, with a myopic outlook on what a successful trader actually is. Successful traders do not strictly measure their success in terms of how much money they made or lost on any particular trade. Successful traders know that they will have many losing streaks lasting days, weeks, and in some cases months. However, in the end they know that they will end up being net winners, because they didn't trade in an egotistical manner.

The vast majority of individuals who start trading will lose money, and many of these traders will define themselves in terms of their actual or perceived profitability. In other words, these individuals will validate their beliefs according to how the market treated them. Typically the beliefs of the conscious mind associate losing money with being a lousy trader, and profitability with being a great trader.

If you are losing money on a particular trade, your beliefs about trading and life may convince you to average down. In this case, your beliefs are preventing you from clearly defining what a winning or losing market position is. Consequently your ego, which is deathly afraid of being wrong once again, will convince you that averaging is the logical thing to do. You can then rationalize away the fact that the position is a loser, because the average cost has been adjusted downward in your favor. This is an example of a myopic belief about the market—namely, that each trade must be a winner. Occasionally averaging down will work, thereby allowing you to avoid the truth. All will go well until averaging down blows up in your face, bankrupting your trading account. All successful traders know that to average down a position is to play with the ultimate demise and ruination of their trading capital.

Are you curious as to why most successful traders at some point early in their careers lose most if not all of their trading capital? The answer is that their beliefs about the market, and what trading is, set them up to lose on a massive scale. That is why many traders buy high and sell low. That is why many novice traders hold on to a losing position *hoping* that it comes back. When presented with a winner, these same novice traders will be quick to take a profit so that they don't give back their hard-won gains. The reason that traders hold on to or average down losers and prematurely offset winners lies in their beliefs! In many cases the impulsive nature of the unconscious mind is not being controlled by the conscious mind. Traders lose their detached, unemotional viewpoint because their beliefs are preventing them from using their rational conscious mind to control their irrational unconscious mind.

Whenever you find yourself fighting the trend, it is because your mind is insisting that it is right and the market is wrong! Whenever you find yourself "hoping" that the market will come around, you are fighting the market. The market never does anything to anyone. It is totally indifferent to you, and your trades. You as a trader are competing only with yourself. In order for you to become the trader you desire, you need to control your thoughts and change your limiting beliefs.

"Hope" is a four-letter word that your ego uses to curse you out.

So how do you change from being an egocentric trader to a trader who accepts the market as it is? In order to change, you need to understand that your mind is only reacting to the events of the outside world, your unconscious desires and thoughts, and your conscious thoughts and desires. Mastering your ego (or self) means strengthening your virtues, values, and beliefs. It also demands that your internal beliefs and their related rules empower your conscious thought process, and therefore powerfully influence the unconscious thought process.

The two strongest virtues that will help your ego balance the demands of your conscious and unconscious minds are integrity and discipline. Integrity allows you to be brutally honest with yourself. Discipline allows you to begin to live and focus in the present moment. When you are able to exist (trade) in the present, you will be able to accurately tell what direction the market is heading. If you enter a trade and have an instant winner, your undisciplined ego feels great; if the trade is an immediate loser, your undisciplined ego makes it hard to do the right thing.

Your gut instinct will be to get rid of the losing trade immediately; however, your ego will generate perfectly valid reasons to hold the losing trade. The correct action is to quickly exit the trade, and take the loss before it gets expensive. However, because of its myopic view of what being a winner is, your ego will prevent you from swallowing your pride (another vice) and exiting the position. Your sense of self will attempt to preserve esteem no matter what the actual consequence is.

How many times have you heard traders say that they don't have a loss until they take it (i.e., it is just a paper loss)? That is their ego talking. It is their ego that allows them to hold on to the losing position until the markets turn around, proving them right. It is their ego stating that *it* is right and the market is wrong. Do you have any idea how much money has been lost because of this reasoning? The logic of not having a loss until it is taken is false; a paper loss is a very real loss. Ask your objective self: "If I honestly feel that it is only a paper loss, why do I feel so bad/angry/disappointed as the price drops? If a paper loss isn't a loss until taken, then a paper profit isn't a profit until taken. So why does it feel so good to have an instant winner?" The primary question asked by all successful traders in the moment is "Do I have a winning or losing trade?" Only novices will ask if they can afford to let the losers accumulate.

Conversely when you have a profitable trade, you often allow your ego to coax you into taking profits quickly. This is because your ego (beliefs) defines success on a trade-by-trade basis, in the shortest possible time frame. Your ego wants and needs the immediate gratification of being right. The ego likes to be correct, and will always be in a state of denial that it is capable of being wrong. It is only after you become aware of the power of an uncontrolled ego to distort reality that you can begin to master it. The first step toward mastery is to become aware of the need to change.

When you as a trader have controlled your ego by changing your beliefs, you will have no fear of being wrong and no burning desire to be "right." You are not hoping, praying, or justifying why the trade should or must work. You are not defining your self-image or self-worth in terms of what the market is doing or how your trades are performing. By not having an "ego" you will be in the present moment, or in the "zone." When you can trade with no ego you become one with the market, much like an expert horseback rider becomes one with the horse.

A successful trader is totally focused on what is happening in the moment. The present moment in time is all that matters in trading and quite probably in life as well. What might happen in the future, or what took place in the past, is totally irrelevant. You as a trader must have the patience to wait for the market to tell you what is taking place in this instant of time. Then you must follow the market by entering it; attempting to interpret why the price is moving is an exercise in futility. Your entire focus should be on how the price is moving right now! Your ego will attempt to interpret what has happened, what is happening, and what should take place in the future. When your ego is correct about the direction of the market, it feels justified and successful—the master of the world. Unfortunately for you, when your ego is wrong, it rationalizes and forgets the wrong beliefs about the direction of the market. All this is very strong justification for starting a trading journal and recording your thoughts and reasoning in it.

Ask yourself: "Once I understand the inner workings of the market, will the market be rational and logical?" Quite naturally almost everyone answers yes. This is expected, because the ego wants it to be so. Ego-driven traders naturally believe that they and they alone will be able to make logical and rational sense out of the market. The truth is that it is impossible to accurately and consistently predict what the market will do next. Yet this is exactly what the ego wants to do. The superior way to trade is to relax and allow the market to tell you if the bears or bulls are in charge. Your ego will fight, resisting the thought that it is best to relax and just let the market reveal itself. The ego wants, and demands, to be in charge. It is diametrically opposed to waiting for the market to unfold so that we may follow. The ego would prefer to anticipate what might happen instead of waiting for the event to take place.

Often the ego will prevent the conscious mind from believing what it is seeing, and will get us to believe what the ego thinks should be happening! This is why we will look at a chart of a commodity that we desperately clung to while it lost increasing amounts of money, before we were eventually forced out, and ask ourselves why we didn't see what was so obvious. Our ego is logically rationalizing the present on the basis of the past, and what it perceives the logical future to be. The ego has an awesome power to exclude from the conscious mind what is actually taking place! To prevent our ego from deluding our conscious mind, we must discipline the ego to focus only on the present moment. *We always get what we focus on.* By using discipline to force us to exist only in the present, without reflection upon the past or anticipation of the future, we will be able to accurately see what is transpiring around us. When we are disciplined to be only in the moment, we will be able to follow the market accordingly.

Once a trader starts to be profitable, the ego wants to accelerate the amount of profits obtained. So the trader will increase the number of contracts traded. Typically the trader who started to be profitable trading one or two contracts will scale up, and begin trading ten contracts. Before long the trader is losing a lot of money. The trader's ego has won the argument that there is no real difference between a one lot and a ten lot. The ego has rationalized away the concept that an incremental increase of one or two contracts might be better than jumping to ten. Everyone's ego is enhanced by size—big house, big car, big bank account, and so on. The ego will always feel better as the size of what is being worked with or desired increases. The trader's ego will argue that the additional risk brought on by more contracts is minuscule and can be ignored. Always remember that the ego is very good at rationalizing and denying reality. Each time out, the ego believes that it is now truly in charge, and that the size of a position really can be increased dramatically without it affecting the trader's judgment.

The ego is extremely averse to pain. If it even slightly suspects that pain is around the corner, it will head in the opposite direction! The ego will procrastinate in taking action as the possibility of pain increases. For example, if you get upset by taking a loss on a one lot, imagine how much pain and effort will be required to exit a ten lot! Without exception, unless you have mastered and actively control your ego, it will hurt a *hundred times* as much, not ten times as much. What keeps you from acting quickly is the fear of pain. The ego is very efficient at justifying the delay and inaction that are required to end this pain. The fear is generated by the ego's attempt to balance the three forces acting upon it.

An unmastered ego will always prevent fast action. Procrastination is caused by the ego, because by quickly taking a loss, the ego is being forced to admit that it is wrong. Outstanding traders are able to exit a losing trade with no hesitation, pain, or effort, because they have mastered their ego. Before you trade a ten lot or hundred lot, you have to make sure that your ego is able to take the increased risk and losses effortlessly. Toddlers learn to run by first taking incremental steps, at a constantly increasing rate, until they are running. The best way to increase the size of the contracts traded is to do so incrementally.

Ego-driven traders absolutely love to show the rest of the world their abilities by picking the bottom or top of a market. Your ego if allowed to will decide that the market is oversold or overbought and should reverse. Since your ego hates to miss a major move, and really detests waiting, it will generate all the reasons in the universe why you must enter right now. Quite naturally your ego wants to demonstrate to itself, and the world, its brilliance and intuitiveness. Your ego wants to enter the trade, and then have the market follow your lead by subsequently reversing direction. The truth of the matter is that you must follow the lead of the market, since the market will very rarely follow your lead.

The largest hindrance you have in consistently making profitable trades is your uncontrolled ego. Your ego will always want to lead the market; it will never want to relax and follow the market. Your ego wants the maximum amount of recognition and glory possible. The best way to achieve glory is by anticipating the future. Consequently the ego becomes very adept at looking at the past and rationalizing what occurred, so that it may anticipate the future. Unless you take the time to master your ego, you will have great difficulty staying in the present moment. Your ego would rather add to a losing trade and, if presented with profits, quickly take them. You can determine if your ego is in charge by asking yourself why you want to buy/hold/exit a position. Is your answer based on past market action, an idea you have logically deduced, resistance to taking a loss right now, fear of letting profits slip through your fingers, a belief that the market must reverse soon, or simply the knowledge that you are right? If so, you can be assured that your ego is in charge.

There are only two situations in which your logical conscious mind can by brute force overpower your ego. Both occur when the period of time you are trading in has elapsed (for example, yesterday for a day trader), and a new time period is just starting (the beginning of a new day). If the price that the market traded at in the previous time period (yesterday) is above the current price, and you are long, then you are losing money; if you are short, then you are making money. In other words, there is no way your ego can deny that truth. Your ego will always do its best to prevent you from responding in a decisive, unhesitating manner.

The ego is nothing more than a sense of self attempting to balance the thoughts of our conscious and unconscious mind. These thoughts are determined by our beliefs and what we value. The two strongest virtues we can call upon to control our ego are discipline and integrity. However, there is another way to gain control of our thoughts. That is to change our beliefs. When we combine our new beliefs with discipline and integrity, we can hasten the speed with which we control our ego. Why do we need to adopt new beliefs or change existing beliefs? To do otherwise will guarantee that we never become the consistently profitable trader we desire.

As noted earlier, our ego is constantly attempting to balance three forces. First, we have our conscious mind, which has rational, unemotional, and emotional thoughts and desires. Second, we have our unconscious mind, which also has desires and thoughts. Third, we have outside events acting on us. These events may or may not be controllable by our actions. They could have a neutral or a large impact on our physical or mental state.

Our unconscious mind will believe vividly imagined events as if they actually took place. It is incapable of telling the difference between what actually occurred and what we only imagined. If the event is imagined only once with enough emotional intensity, the unconscious mind may remember it forever. Likewise if an event is imagined repeatedly but with a low level of emotional intensity, it too may be remembered forever. The more vividly we can imagine an event using all five of our senses, the more real it becomes; and as the emotional intensity increases, the event has a greater and greater impact on our unconscious minds. Although our conscious mind can be controlled by our beliefs, our unconscious mind is totally and absolutely uncontrollable—because it is perceiving things that our conscious mind fails to perceive.

Our unconscious mind is very aware of the events that we are experiencing and the thoughts that arise in our conscious mind. For example, in the 1960s drive-in movie theaters flashed the words "eat popcorn" and "drink Coke" as subliminal messages on the movie screen. Our unconscious mind was aware of the message even though our conscious mind was not. In a lot of ways our unconscious mind and our conscious mind act as filters for the information that passes in both directions. Our unconscious mind shapes conscious thought, and our conscious mind influences our unconscious. As we shall shortly see, our unconscious mind is constantly attempting to meet certain needs and desires. By using our conscious mind, we can generate thoughts that influence our unconscious mind. In this manner we can increase our level of creative and intuitive thought.

As we master our ego we are actually mastering our conscious thoughts, our unconscious desires or thoughts, and our perception of outside events. Mastery of our mind comes from awareness that there must be a change in our beliefs. Successful traders know that they have mastered their ego when they are able to suspend judgment and conscious thought while trading. In short, while trading they are in the zone, though unaware of being there.

In many sports competitions, the participants are totally unaware of their surroundings or what they are actually doing. Motorcycle racers are truly oblivious to their environment and completely focused on the present moment. Mentally they are not reflecting on the accident that occurred back in turn four, or on the victory dinner scheduled for that evening. There is no fear because they are existing in the present moment. If asked after the race is over, they would say that they were one with the motorcycle and the racetrack. In short, they were in the zone. Similarly, many successful pit traders will tell you that their most profitable days are days when they are in the zone. In other words, a trader in the zone is trading in the present moment, at one with the market, and oblivious to everything else. While existing in the zone, the trader has no ego, has suspended conscious thought, and has adopted the thoughts of the market.

THE POWER OF BELIEFS

It is our beliefs that determine what we value most in life, the character traits we live by, and our ultimate destiny. Every individual has a multitude of beliefs. We have beliefs about love, success, failure, happiness, anger, resentment, contribution, driving a car, raising children—in short, every emotion or activity possible. As traders we have beliefs about the meaning of a divergence, double bottoms, rising moving averages, increasing volume, advance/decline ratios, hammers, and so on. Our beliefs are what our conscious mind uses to interpret the events that it perceives. *A belief is nothing more than a feeling of certainty about what an event or feeling means to us.* Beliefs exist in our conscious and unconscious mind, and their validity is not questioned.

When we were children, our beliefs came from the role models in our lives, mainly our parents. As youngsters, we adopted their beliefs about what different events and feelings meant. Beliefs about love, sadness, and humor come primarily to mind. At that point in our lives the only reference points we had were our parents. When we entered school we suddenly had more role models (teachers or our peer group); these expanded references allowed us to come up with additional beliefs. As we began to mature, we experienced new events that caused us either pain or pleasure. These new experiences led our mind to look for a cause, how recent it was, and if we had consistently felt this way in the past. Our mind then evaluated the validity of the event and whether it met our four primary needs, which are:

1. The need for a feeling of certainty.
2. The need for a feeling of variety.
3. The need to feel significant.
4. The need to feel that we are loved and connected to others.

We then took the new belief, based on the reference (or event), and incorporated it into our conscious and unconscious mind. For example, as we began to date we discovered that kissing was highly enjoyable (mentally and physically). Our mind experienced pleasure, and then began looking for the most recent "event" connected to the pleasure. The most recent connected to pleasure was the physical act of kissing. Our mind concluded that the act of kissing is what caused the pleasure. Our mind then attempted to determine if we consistently got pleasure when we kissed. After determining that we did consistently obtain pleasure by kissing, our mind needed to evaluate the validity that kissing was pleasurable by determining if kissing met our four primary needs. If it did meet these needs, then the mind would conclude that kissing was a pleasurable activity. In other words, the need for certainty would be met if every time a kiss was experienced it was pleasurable; the need of variety would be fulfilled if there were a wide variety of kisses; the need for significance would be fulfilled if kissing made us feel significant to the other person; and the need for love and connection would be met if while kissing the other person the feeling of love and personal connection was experienced. Since all four needs were met, the mind decided to believe that kissing was pleasurable. Our mind also constructed certain rules with our belief. Such a rule might have been that kissing our dog would not be enjoyable or that kissing someone with bad breath would not be enjoyable.

That is why almost everyone experiences or believes there's pleasure in kissing. Likewise, as we kiss we begin to link pleasure to a person's face. Consequently every time we see that person (assuming there has been no painful argument), we link pleasure consciously and unconsciously to his or her face. This association occurs because our mind is certain that kissing the face is pleasurable, that the person kisses in a variety of ways, and that significance is experienced as well as love and connection.

Of course, in another person's belief system, our significant other—the object of our affection—could be a source of pain. Suppose that the person of our affection is consistently mean to Pat, a coworker. Soon Pat will have a belief that our significant other causes pain. This is because whenever Pat sees that person, pain follows. If Pat is insulted, let's say immediately after seeing that person's face, Pat's mind will begin to link pain to the face. As Pat's mind evaluates the cause—that pain immediately follows seeing that person's face and being spoken to, and that the pain is consistently felt—it concludes with a perfectly valid belief that seeing the person's face is painful. This is just the opposite of our belief!

Allow me to ask you a question. If every time you received information that someone you cared about had died came from a phone call after 11 p.m., do you think you would begin to believe that phone calls after 11 p.m. are always bad? Why? *The way our mind creates beliefs is of vital importance to us as we change our own beliefs and create new ones.* This is why some traders experience massive pain whenever the market creates a gap, while other traders anticipate great joy. Ultimately as new traders begin losing increasing amounts of money, they form a belief that the methodology they are using is the culprit. They will then buy multiple trading programs in the hope of finding a "painless" one. In reality, of course, their beliefs are causing the pain. The pain is self-inflicted!

Another interesting thing about beliefs is that the physical or emotional state that we are in when we experience a new event or point of reference will strongly influence both our perception of that event and how our beliefs about that event are shaped.

The market is able to inflict massive pain on traders only because their beliefs about themselves and the market are being violated. The mind is constantly attempting to meet its four primary needs. One of the many beliefs held by novice traders is that the market can be predicted once it is understood—so they have a feeling of certainty. Most novice traders find significance by being a "trader." Consequently the market can inflict massive pain on novice traders because of their false beliefs in certainty and significance. The truth of the matter is that the market is unpredictable in an absolute sense, and the market will never provide certainty. The certainty must come from the trader. The market will provide all the variety a trader could desire, so it does meet one of the four primary needs. The market will never provide significance or connection. So of the four primary needs, only one is being met. This is why you as a trader must become aware of the power of your beliefs and change them so that they serve you.

There are four types of beliefs that people possess. The first type is an *opinion*. We link low levels of energy to our opinions, and we're relatively certain that we are right—but we're not absolutely certain. When we have an opinion we will discuss its validity without getting overly upset. The second type of belief is what we normally call a *belief*. We link low to medium levels of emotional intensity to most of our beliefs. Unlike an opinion, we are absolutely certain that a given belief is valid, and we're close-minded about its validity. If someone challenges our belief and/or its validity, we tend to get upset. The third type of belief is a *conviction*. A conviction has a high level of emotional intensity linked to it. We are absolutely certain that our conviction is correct, and if our conviction is questioned we immediately get angry and defensive. The fourth type of belief is a *rule*. We use rules to determine if the virtues, vices, and emotional feelings that we value most are being met. We link a lot of emotional intensity to our rules. We are absolutely certain that they are valid, and we become upset if they are questioned. The important thing to remember about beliefs is that they can either empower or disempower our lives.

Our beliefs dynamically impact our unconscious mind, our character traits, and the vehicles we use to realize our values. Our beliefs will powerfully influence the quality of the desires, thoughts, and intuitive ideas generated by our unconscious mind. Likewise, our beliefs impact the character traits that we as individuals rely on in our daily lives. Faith, confidence, discipline, courage, persistence, flexibility, integrity, and honesty, are all character traits that we call upon in our daily lives. Our beliefs will determine the language we use with others and with ourselves. Beliefs dictate whether we treat others with love and respect or with anger and hostility. Our beliefs influence how we move our bodies (posture, breathing, laughing). Perhaps most important, our beliefs determine how we obtain and perceive new information. Consequently our behavior is determined by our beliefs. Our behavior is how we express our human emotions and beliefs. The way we behave and interact with the market as traders is determined by the beliefs we possess about the market and our lives.

Our beliefs determine what we value most in our lives. *Our values are emotional feelings that we hold to be most important in all areas of life.* We would naturally like to experience these desirable values on a daily basis. Those values that we want to move toward are typically love, happiness, health, passion, intelligence, significance, success, contribution, freedom, gratefulness, and achievement—all values that enrich our lives. We can also have emotional feelings that we do not want to experience. These are our "moving away from" values, and typically they are feelings of anger, failure, disappointment, loneliness, hate, despair, resentment, and other negative feelings.

All too often when people are asked what they value most in their lives, they answer with the "vehicles" they value. What people think they value most is only a "vehicle" that their conscious or unconscious mind uses to meet what it actually values the most. In other words, the mind is using a vehicle to obtain what it wants. It is our beliefs that determine what vehicle we use to obtain what we value, and need.

A vehicle is what we use to obtain what we actually value or need.

For example, if we ask four different individuals what they value most, they might answer: "My Mercedes and my home." "The ability to beat the crap out of an opponent." "My ability to give love and compassion to another." "My ability to provide extraordinary insights into the market." Depending upon their beliefs, they could *all* value the same emotional feeling. Do you care to hazard a guess on what that may be?

The first person mentions her Mercedes and house. The truth of the matter is that the material possessions are giving her an emotional feeling that often equates with significance. She is using material possessions to feel significant. The second person is using violence against others (or himself) to fulfill their need of significance. The third person uses compassion and love to obtain the feeling of significance. The fourth person is using extraordinary levels of skill and knowledge to achieve significance. Each person is actually valuing significance; however, all are using different vehicles to accomplish that feeling. The purpose of this example is to show that in order to accomplish what you value most in life, you need to become aware of the underlying reasons for your actions. If you as a trader value your unique trading methodology, ask yourself whether it is a vehicle for something else.

The vehicles that we use in our daily lives include controlling others or events, consistently doing or thinking the same thing, faith (often part of religion), alcohol (often abuse), drugs (often abuse), food, changing jobs, moving, tearing others down, violence, material possessions, academic degrees, contribution, caring, compassion, gangs, sex, and joining a team. All of these are different vehicles we use to obtain what we value or need.

Some of the vehicles we use as traders are computers and related computer programs: back-testing and optimization of our trading methodologies; and three different forms of analysis: mental analysis, fundamental analysis, and technical analysis. The futility of using a vehicle to accomplish what we value is that we mistakenly believe that it is mastery or ownership of the vehicle that we really desire. In actuality we want mastery of something else entirely.

All traders, whether novice or professional, place a high value on the feeling of certainty. Unfortunately the vast majority of novice traders fall into the trap of believing that by using a computer (a vehicle) and purchasing an expensive trading program (another vehicle), they will be able to accomplish what they value—namely, certainty. Other traders in an attempt to achieve certainty will talk to as many different traders (a vehicle) as possible. Still other traders (most professionals) will work toward certainty by focusing on their mental abilities and controlling their emotional states. These traders know that they will always act in their best interests with no fear or hesitation. The vehicle here is internal beliefs, and their associated rules.

The interesting thing to keep in mind is that the thoughts and desires of the unconscious mind will also influence your character traits, your behavior, and the vehicles you use to accomplish what you value most. All aspects of your mental, physical, and spiritual abilities are impacted by your beliefs. The ultimate goal of your beliefs is to obtain certainty, variety, significance, loving connection, growth, and a sense of contribution, and what you value most in your life.

CHANGING A BELIEF

Remember that beliefs are nothing more than feelings of certainty about what different events mean. They exist in our conscious and unconscious mind, and they are not normally questioned. Our beliefs originate from our life experiences, references, and events as we perceive them. Our perception is influenced by our beliefs and the physical and emotional state that we were in while perceiving certain events. In order to change our beliefs we need to understand a little bit more about points of reference. As we know, references can be real events or imagined ones, or they can be derived from other people (i.e., role models). As we go through life we experience many different events. Our mind interprets and organizes these references in a manner that will either empower or disempower us. All too often, because of our beliefs, the mind interprets these events in a disempowering manner.

The first step is to make a conscious decision to change your existing beliefs by altering your perception of your life experiences in an empowering way. The mind interprets and gives meaning to everything you experience. That interpretation and perception is influenced by your beliefs, values, and expectations.

One tool you can use to interpret new events in an empowering way is contrast. By contrasting any new experience with a less desirable experience, you can change your perceptions and feelings in such a way as to create an empowering belief. For example, if as a trader you are stopped out of a trade and incur a loss, and subsequently the market reverses—a shift that would have generated a profit if you had not used a stop—you can use contrast to change the experience from a negative one to a less negative and possibly positive one. You could contrast the small loss experienced by using a stop with the large loss experienced by a different trader (a reference) or by yourself at another time when a stop was not used.

The second step is that you must obtain more references. For many traders, new references wind up costing a lot of money. This is why determining the references of other traders and then using them is so beneficial to your bottom line. As we obtain more references, we have more choices available to us, and our faith increases that we will accomplish what we desire. We can also obtain more references by reexamining our own life experiences. Often a negative or painful experience will have an empowering lesson embedded in it. If we remember it as we normally would, our physiology will reflect the amount of pain (mental or physical) that we were experiencing. In such a state it becomes very difficult to perceive that experience in a way that we could learn and grow from it. However, if we remember the experience while in a peak physiological state, and while asking questions that change our focus, our perception of the event may change enough so that we are able to learn something that empowers us.

For example, if you had the misfortune a few months ago to be long when hogs went limit down for five consecutive days, the amount of pain you experienced might have been immense. If you remember that experience as you normally would, it is doubtful that you will learn anything from it. However, by changing your physiology so that it is in a peak state, and then remembering the event, and asking yourself empowering questions, you greatly enhance your chances of gaining a new, positive perspective. So how do you change your physiology? Easy! If you want to change your physiology so that it is totally confident, then ask yourself a question. "Can I remember a time that I had total certainty that I could accomplish any task? Can I remember a time that I was totally confident of my abilities?" Then as you remember those experiences from your past, take the time to fully remember each event using all five senses. What were you seeing, hearing, feeling, touching, and smelling? The last step is to adopt the same physiology as you had then. Breathe, move, and speak the same way. Now you have the physiology of a confident person. What happens if you have never felt totally certain? If you are sure that you have never experienced a feeling of certainty, then find a good role model and adopt his or her physiology. Alan Greenspan comes to mind. When he goes on stage, does he move like he is doubtful? Of course not. He is absolutely certain about his outcome.

Now that you have changed your physiology into a confident state, ask yourself questions that will help you perceive the event differently. With the limit-down market experience, you might ask: "Was the market attempting to give me information that I ignored? How might I have interpreted the market action so as to exit the long position before the market went limit down? Was there a way I could have hedged or offset my loss in a different market? How did I behave? If there was a valuable lesson in this experience, what was it? How might I decrease my overall risk of being caught in a limit move in the future?" Your goal in asking yourself questions is to change your perception of the event enough so that you can learn something valuable about it. The pain you experienced will remain; however, by learning something valuable from the experience, you can perhaps lessen the pain.

Whenever we reexperience an event while we are in a peak state, our perception improves. This is why we will often find a nugget of wisdom that was overlooked initially. We can also obtain more references by using our imagination. Imagination is ten times more powerful than willpower. By using our imagination, we can provide our mind with a clear vision and certainty. The secret of references is that the more we get that empower us, the better we become at evaluating references. The more our evaluation process improves, the higher the quality of our decisions. In addition, as we obtain more references, we become better at living life and experiencing empowering feelings.

The third step in changing a belief is to change the physical and emotional state you are in. When you change your physical and emotional state, you are changing your ability to perceive new information. Your physiology has a gigantic impact on what emotional state you are in. You will never see the winner of a race walking into the winner's circle with poor physiology (shallow breathing, poor posture, slouching shoulders, etc.). Likewise you will very rarely see a person who was just fired from a desirable job walk out of the building as if she just won $1 million. The physiology of the loser is totally opposite the physiology of a winner. It is the physiology that determines the body's ability to obtain oxygen and circulate the blood. A person with poor physiology is unable to physically maintain the body. Consequently the mental ability to perceive and focus on new information is impaired. The emotional state is also impaired. This is the beginning of a vicious circle: As the emotional state deteriorates, it affects the physiology even more.

When we change our physiology, we're able to change our perception. As our physiology and perception begin to change, our emotional state will also begin to change, allowing us to perceive even more information. As our perception increases, we can begin to examine the references that made up our beliefs and then ask intelligent questions. Our previous perception will then begin to change, because the underlying beliefs are beginning to change. Soon we introduce some doubt about the validity of our original perception of the reference.

The fourth step in changing a belief is to change your perception of the underlying reference. Your perception is altered by asking probing questions that access more of your innate intelligence. Questions also change your focus, which will affect how you feel and what you think. Since the mind deletes or ignores the vast majority of what it experiences, asking questions helps you become aware of what is being or has been deleted. When you change your perception of the underlying reference, you begin to form new beliefs that cast doubt on the original perception.

The fifth and last step is to make a *decision* that these new beliefs are valid. The ability to decide is a quality that too few people possess.

For example, let us look at a novice trader who believes that all it takes to make millions is $5000 in trading capital, a $3000 computer, and a $4000 trading program. The trader can change this belief (assuming that he wants to) by determining what references he is using to sustain that belief. Say that our trader has two points of reference: reading about several traders who turned $10,000 into $1 million, and looking over various ads in the trading magazines. By placing himself into a peak physiological state and a peak emotional state, our trader will be ready to examine his references. Then, by asking intelligent questions, he will either validate his initial belief or introduce doubt, thereby allowing the creation of a new belief. He will change the focus of his mind. Often he will become aware of much of what his unconscious has been deleting, and he will be able to access more mental and physical resources.

Let's look at some of the questions our trader could ask: "How many years of experience did the traders who turned $10,000 into $1 million have? How many times has it been done? If it was so easy, why hasn't it happened more often? How many trading methodologies did the trader discard before finding the successful one? If the computer program makes so much money, why is it for sale? If it does make money, how many traders can use it before it loses its effectiveness? If a $3000 computer running Microsoft Windows is adequate for making millions, why do the large hedge funds have $30,000 workstations? If a data feed that cost $300 a month will make me millions, why do the top CTAs have data feeds that cost thousands of dollars every month? What information am I failing to see? Ten years from now if I reexamined this issue, what new information would I see? What belief would empower me? What belief would allow me to see more information?"

These are just some of the questions that would enable our novice trader to see the fallacy of his original belief. As our trader answers these questions, he will begin to realize that perhaps his old beliefs were not reflecting reality. At this point he must make a *decision* that the old beliefs were erroneous, and that he will create new beliefs that more accurately portray reality.

Let us look at another novice trader who believes that ultimately she will become a successful trader. Since she is a novice, she has no actual trading references. Consequently all her beliefs regarding trading are based on the references of other traders. The vast majority of these beliefs were obtained from reading books, watching videos, and attending seminars. In order for our novice trader to obtain valid beliefs about the markets, she must first start asking intelligent questions. She must carefully choose as references other traders who are producing consistent profits. She must vividly imagine to the best of her ability that these valid references are her own, so that she will obtain her own empowering beliefs.

Let's look at some of the questions our second novice trader might ask: "Is there a common methodology for all successful traders? If so, what is it? If there is no common methodology, is there something else that all successful traders have in common? If the vast majority of new traders lose money, what are they focusing on? What materials are they studying? What aspects of trading do the vast majority of new traders mentally delete? Why am I really trading? What value of mine am I attempting to fulfill through trading? Can I fulfill it without trading? If I could ask the best trader in the world (alive or dead) for advice, what would I ask and what would I imagine the answer to be? What references could I imagine that this great trader would have?"

Six months is the average life expectancy of most commodity traders. They will lose so much money that they become disgusted and quit trading. In other words, it takes them six months to adopt beliefs that are so disempowering—that attach so much pain to trading—that the traders abandon the beliefs that originally got them into the market. Then for the rest of their lives they have their "war stories" to tell friends and family members. The vast majority of traders and people in general do not have the determination to take control of their ego or their belief structure. Many times you will know the right thing to do, in trading or in life, yet be unable to follow through. Always remember that it is your beliefs that are causing the hesitation. Often the hesitation occurs because your beliefs or values are themselves in conflict. Hesitation will always arise when discipline is lacking. Once you begin to understand the power that your beliefs hold over you, your newfound awareness will help you slowly overcome that power. Until you master your ego, it will continue to behave in a very egotistical manner—much like a self-centered child. Your ego will always demand instant gratification. In fact, your ego will become very upset if gratification in the present moment is delayed even to achieve dramatically more gratification in the future.

As you read about the other virtues and beliefs in the rest of this book, and how important they are for the excellent trader, always keep in mind how they can help you create more empowering beliefs. Discipline is perhaps the best virtue to call upon in mastering your mental abilities. As you begin to realize how your mind creates a multitude of problems in your personal and trading life, you will become even more committed to controlling your mind by creating valid, effective, and empowering rules. As your level of understanding about the importance of virtues increases, remember that the largest vice a trader will confront is egotism caused by invalid beliefs. The other typical vices that must also be overcome are anger, resentment, greed, doubt, and fear. As you begin to trade with more effective beliefs, you will discover that the struggle eases. When your ego has been mastered and your belief structure is in place, you will be able to see, hear, and feel what the market is attempting to tell you.

Another tool that you may find beneficial in controlling your ego is to practice yoga or learn how to meditate. I practice Zazen mediation, yoga, and playing GO. The discipline of all three helps strengthen the desirable parts of my ego and annihilate the undesirable ones. As your ability to discipline your mind increases, your equity will increase as well. Disciplining your mind is a never-ending process.

Without mastery of your ego and your beliefs, you are building your trading success on sand.

3

FAITH: THE FOUNDATION OF ALL OUTSTANDING TRADERS

The belief that becomes truth for me…is that which allows me the best use of my strength, the best means of putting my virtues into action.

—ANDRÉ GIDE

As he thinketh in his heart, so is he.

—PROVERBS 23:7

Y**OU MUST BE THINKING** "Wow, I have read a lot of trading books, and I never heard anyone mention faith before." A lot of what we accomplish in life is based on some pretty simple truths. Let's think about faith for a second. Everything we accomplish is anchored in our faith that we possess, or will possess, the skills necessary to accomplish our goals. Faith is the foundation of all human endeavors. When most people think of faith, they think of religion. This because all religions require their faithful to possess it. Faith is an integral part of spiritual belief; a religion without faith would not be a religion. Faith is also an integral part of every individual. The more faith an individual trader possesses, the more he or she will accomplish. Faith is perhaps one of the highest forms of belief a person can possess—it is a conviction.

Faith is absolutely essential to modern society. Without it, civilization would cease to exist! If you started to drive to work and everyone was driving around in a frenzy, your level of faith or certainty that you would arrive at work without an accident would plummet toward zero! If no one was stopping for red lights, if cars were going the wrong way on the roads, if some people were driving backward, and so on, the level of certainty that you previously had would be gone.

In order for people to drive to work in a reasonable time (if at all), they must be fairly certain that the traffic laws will be obeyed by everyone else. If this was not true, then traffic would be very slow—stop and go—and crazy. In other words, the drivers on the road must have a *consensus* that the traffic laws of today are the same as the laws of yesterday. How do you think this applies to trading?

Let me give you another example. Can you remember a time in your life when you wanted to do something with real desire, and yet it seemed like you would never get the hang of it? Perhaps it was arguing a case before a jury, performing surgery, or participating in a sport like golf or skiing. After a lot of practice, you did eventually master and perhaps even excel at the activity. Do you remember some of the beliefs that you possessed that empowered you to take the first steps in mastering that skill?

Do you think that faith was one of them? You bet! If people had no sense of faith that they could learn to snowboard, for example, do you honestly think that they would ever rent a snowboard and take that first plunge down the mountain on a very slick surface? Of course not! Again, how do you think this applies to you at trading?

Have you ever wondered about the difference between the Sunday golfer and the professional? What belief did the professional have that the amateur didn't?

I would like to submit that a major factor was the level of faith. The professional had more faith in excelling at the sport than did the amateur. This enabled the professional to endure more training, more pain, more punishment to the body and the ego. People who lack faith are unable to overcome the hardships that life presents. They succumb to the challenges that they encounter, and never accomplish the success that they seek.

As Hannibal said, "We will either find a way or make a way." His level of faith (and certainty) was extremely high. All outstanding leaders have always believed that they would eventually accomplish their goal. They were always certain that the outcome would be as expected. They might have not known *how* they would accomplish their goal, but they knew that they would accomplish it. Thomas Edison performed more than 10,000 experiments before finally succeeding with the incandescent light bulb. He had faith that eventually he would figure out how to build an incandescent bulb. He also believed that every experiment that failed to produce light was valuable nonetheless. Although the outcome was not what he desired, he felt that he obtained valuable insight into what to do (or not do) in the next experiment.

Another analogy is to an airplane pilot. Upon departing from the airport, the pilot is certain that his plane will arrive at its intended destination. He has faith that the procedures and training that he and his crew have mastered will get them to their goal. Did you ever think about how often the airline captain, and the autopilot, needs to adjust the direction of the airplane? Regardless of storms and high winds, the certainty of the pilot remains unwavering—because of faith.

Trading is the same. Great traders always have total faith that regardless of what the markets do, they will accomplish their goal. Do great traders have total certainty on where prices are going? No. How could they? Yet great traders have faith that their methodology and belief structure will in the end allow them to reach their goal. How is this possible? Outstanding traders are certain that the methodology they have so painstakingly researched will generate occasional losses, that the markets will be choppy, that the finance ministers of the world will cause the markets to be volatile, and so on. Through it all the faith that they will triumph remains steadfast.

Let's say you are a stock trader and you follow IBM. How do you know when there is overwhelming "continuity of thought" about where the price of IBM is heading? Easy. The price is going straight up or down—the trend is clearly identifiable. Likewise you know that there is no continuity of thought when the market is very choppy—when it is going sideways.

The concept of "continuity of thought" is quite simple. When the opinion of the majority of traders comes to a consensus, the market will begin trending. At this point the continuity of thought of the market (or the majority of the traders) enables the trend to continue. In other words, if the majority of traders have faith that prices are cheap right now, and that prices will be higher in the future, then they will continue thinking that prices are heading higher—until some event happens to change their continuity of bullish thought.

When the available pool of investor/traders for a particular market is expressing a certain continuity of thought, profit making becomes easier. Traders who have faith that their methodology will allow them to enter into a trade at the right time will always over time be more profitable than traders who have little faith in their methodology.

How do you create faith and certainty in the trading environment? You start out by realizing how critical faith is in your everyday life. You start looking at group interactions (obtaining more references), and how faith or the lack thereof speeds up or delays the interaction or ultimate goal of the group. Understand that faith is a belief that you possess, and only you can generate faith and certainty for yourself. I cannot give it to you, nor can you buy it—you must generate it on your own.

When you have faith that an intended goal will eventually be accomplished, you have taken the first step. Every time you acknowledge how important faith is, how often you use it every day, you are strengthening your belief system. You must realize how you rely on faith every day, in every activity you do, and how critical it is in learning new things. Faith and certainty are both beliefs, and as with a muscle, the more you use a belief the stronger it becomes.

As we discussed earlier, you can modify your existing beliefs so that they empower you; you can also come up with entirely new beliefs that will empower you. This approach applies to faith as well. The first step is to get into a peak physiological and emotional state. As you think about faith, do any role models pop into your mind who had huge amounts of faith? How do you think these individuals became so powerful in faith? What references did they have? Did they have a consistent physical and emotional state? What references can you imagine that they imagined they had? Next reexamine some of your own references while remaining in peak physiological and emotional state. What references did you use when you called upon faith in the past? What questions can you ask now to clarify what you are focusing on by expanding their resources? These are just some of the questions you can ask to modify and expand your beliefs about faith.

When you have faith about accomplishing a goal, you have removed all doubt. This is because people who have faith also possess certainty. Doubt is the opposite of certainty. Doubt (a vice) will cause traders to overanalyze the market and the methodology they developed. Certainty removes doubt, and creates profits. This sounds simple, and it is. However, it takes faith to create certainty.

You must use faith to become certain that your ability as a trader and your trading methodology will ultimately enable you to arrive at your goal. Currently you may not know exactly how you will get there, but you must become certain that you will eventually succeed. It is vitally important that you understand that as you increase faith and develop certainty, your ability as a trader will continue to improve, eventually guaranteeing your triumph.

In other words, airplane pilots will retain their faith and level of certainty about arriving at their intended destination regardless of the obstacles en route. They may have to take a detour around a large storm, but they will eventually land safely. Just as the level of certainty of the airline pilot is unwavering, so your level of certainty as a trader must remain unwavering.

Faith breeds confidence, success, and certainty. Faith fights doubt and uncertainty, which lead to fear, doubt, despair, disappointment, and hesitation. Faith will overcome the four primary obstacles that all traders encounter. The first obstacle is the trader's mind. It is in the mind where our abilities reside, and where beliefs and values exist. Faith will overcome any limiting values and beliefs. The second obstacle is fundamental analysis. Regardless of our trading abilities, there's always some fundamental aspect about the markets that we lack information about or lack understanding of. The third obstacle is technical analysis. As with fundamental analysis, regardless of the abilities of the trader there will always be a new and perhaps more efficient way to perceive the markets technically. The fourth obstacle is the markets themselves. Markets can be unpredictable and inconsistent, and they possess endless variations. The trader who possesses faith will overcome all these obstacles.

Your goal in creating faith in your trading abilities is to know that you will overcome all obstacles, and that you will eventually become a very profitable trader. It is a matter not of *if* you become a profitable trader, but *when.* It is your faith, and developing a sense of certainty about yourself and your trading ability, that will allow you to learn, research, and apply what you learn to trading. Currently you have a lot of beliefs that involve faith and certainty in your everyday life. You must add trading to this list.

Faith is the foundation that all other virtues are built upon. It is absolutely essential to a trader's ultimate success. Outstanding traders have a multitude of certain beliefs: that the market action will be unpredictable, that their methodology is valid, that the methodology will still create losses, that losses can result from market inefficiencies and lack of continuity of thought, that every loss and profit holds valuable information, and most important that they will triumph because of their faith that they are excellent traders.

One word of caution. Certainty can become a vice if it is generated by the ego. For example, you suddenly become certain that pork bellies are going to go up in the next few months. The way to determine that such a feeling of certainty is a vice, generated by the ego, is to realize that the conviction is dependent upon someone else or an action controlled by others. If your certainty is based upon and dependent upon your actions, then it is a strong virtue grounded in faith.

As your level of certainty in your ability as a trader increases, the role played by your ego will begin to diminish. Faith will combat and eliminate doubt.

CONFIDENCE IS REQUIRED FOR SUCCESS

The key is consistency and discipline. Almost anybody can make up a list of rules that are 80% as good as what we taught. What they can't do is give [people] the confidence to stick to those rules even when things are going bad.

—RICHARD DENNIS

There are two things that are absolutely critical: You must have confidence, and you have to be willing to make mistakes regularly; there is nothing wrong with it.

—BRUCE KOVNER

CONFIDENCE IS THE second virtue that all outstanding traders must possess. Confidence is a belief whose foundation lies in faith. Faith is based on a definite conviction that an ultimate outcome will be achieved. Outstanding traders have faith that they will make a profit over time. They have faith that their methodology will work over the long haul. They are confident *because* of their faith that they will achieve their ultimate outcome, that their methodology will evolve to the point where it is profitable. Their confidence is also derived from all the research (a reference, and a vehicle) they conducted to develop their methodology. These traders obtained their confidence *after* they had faith that they would triumph. Granted this is a subtle difference; however, it is a critical difference.

When traders have faith that they will triumph, their level of confidence dramatically rises. They can then develop and refine their trading methodology until it is profitable. Their confidence is derived from their references about their own abilities and the abilities of others.

Many novice traders have faith in the computer program they purchased or the newsletter they are subscribing to. This faith then gives them confidence based upon their reference about the validity of the program or newsletter, which depends on how successfully the marketing department presented the material. Their confidence is based not on their abilities as traders, but on the abilities of the copywriters for the advertisement. The confidence of novice traders is also based on their ego, which convinces them that the computer program or newsletter is worthwhile. This confidence is shattered after they get a margin call or realize that their account is down 50 percent. It is shattered because the feeling of confidence generated by the copywriters has been negated by the reality of the marketplace. When a belief is violated, negative emotions result. The purpose of the advertisements is to generate feelings of faith, by giving us what we believe are valid references. This allows our mind to convince us that our belief of certainty is valid. However, as we learned in the previous chapter, if the feeling of certainty is created or dependent upon the action of others, it is probably the result of an uncontrolled ego.

Other new traders are able to see the fallacy in newsletters and prewritten trading programs, and decide to purchase a computer software that allows them to write their own program. By now you know that it is their ego telling them that they can write a program, and become fabulously wealthy from trading it in the next six months. After all, they and they alone have the unique ability to write the winning program! Once again, their confidence is derived from the feeling of certainty generated by their ego.

That confidence will be shattered when they have to wire more money to their account after their superbly written trading program blows up.

The point that I am striving to make is that in order to have genuine confidence, a trader has to ground that confidence in faith. If the feeling of confidence is being created by the trader's ego, then the confidence is in fact false. The confidence that most new traders possess is based on nothing more than quicksand. In other words, the confidence is built upon *f*alse *e*vidence that *a*ppears *r*eal. That is correct for those of you sharp enough to catch it. FEAR. It is the ego operating from a state of fear that generates the illusion of confidence. Most novice traders, told that their confidence is based upon this illusion, would vehemently deny it. However, in almost all cases everything a novice trader does is based on fear. Fear in all cases is evidence (references) that appear real but that are in actuality false. In most cases the evidence presented consists of untested beliefs (our own or others), untested/invalid trading methodologies (our own or others), and references that have not been validated. Confidence is an illusion if it is not founded upon faith in our own references. It is an illusion if it comes from our ego, and involves arrogance and conceit.

Confidence must be built on the virtue of faith, and in order for that to happen you must acknowledge how your ego is distorting your perceptions of reality. The level of confidence needed to become an outstanding trader is based on a deep inner conviction of faith that your abilities, and ultimate methodology, will triumph in time. When you have real confidence in your ability as a trader, you will not care what *anyone* else says about the market direction. Real confidence will allow you to have the persistence to remain with *your* trading methodology. Your level of confidence will allow you to base your trading perspective on your own research. In fact, when Richard Dennis taught his novice traders—a group who would later be called the "Turtles"—he always asked them a simple question to see if they understood. The question was basically along these lines: "If your methodology is telling you to get short sugar tomorrow on the open, and you find out this evening over dinner that I am getting long sugar tomorrow on the open, what do you do?" The only correct answer is "I would still go short sugar on the open." That is real confidence derived from faith, with the ego in check.

Allow me to ask you a question: Are you confident that you can drive your car to the dry cleaner? In any type of weather? Of course you are. Why? Is it perhaps your level of faith that derives from your confidence is based upon your own valid references? Would you be interested in having me tell you over the next six pages how to drive there? Why not?

The outstanding trader will have the exact same belief for the same exact reasons concerning trading as you have about driving to the dry cleaner. You will not care if it is sunny or rainy, or if there is a snowstorm in progress, for you know that you will eventually get to the dry cleaner regardless. You are not going to consult the weather channel, read a book, or subscribe to a fax service on the best route to take. Nor will you waste your time talking with your neighbors about driving to the dry cleaner.

The reason is that you have confidence in your ability to drive to the dry cleaner. That confidence is founded upon your *faith in your outcome*. Further, your references reinforce your feeling of confidence. An outstanding trader will have the same belief about trading. An outstanding trader will not care about what others are thinking, what the fax services are saying, or how "stormy" the markets are. All outstanding traders have a deep-seated confidence in their ability to overcome every challenge the market might present. That confidence allows them to consistently apply the trading methodology they have developed. Their confidence is founded upon the certainty that they will achieve their desired outcome.

How do you develop the confidence to consistently trade your own, unique trading methodology? Easy! Since confidence is a belief, it can be obtained (if lacking), changed (if disempowering), and increased by using the techniques on changing a belief previously covered. Just remember that confidence implies faith in your own beliefs and abilities. It also implies that your ego is controlled—that is, your confidence has no conceit mixed in with it.

Your confidence level will increase after you have started to control your ego. Confidence is strengthened when you realize that you and you alone must have faith to devise your own trading methodology. Your trading methodology will reflect your unique perceptions and beliefs. Your trading methodology is how you as a trader interpret the action of the market. It is how you identify the trends, reversals, and market indecision. It is how you enter and exit the market and how you know that your trade should be exited.

The really important thing to remember is that before you can begin to develop and gain confidence in a trading methodology, you must have faith that you will achieve the outcome that you desire. You must have faith in your abilities to develop an effective trading methodology. Confidence gives you increased levels of discipline, persistence, and faith. Confidence also gives you valid references, methodologies, and beliefs.

Without confidence you will not have the ability to implement all the other virtues that becoming an excellent trader demands. Confidence in your abilities will give you the perseverance to continue developing your abilities as a trader. Learning to control your ego, while having faith that you will accomplish your outcome, will give you the confidence you need to succeed.

5

DISCIPLINED TRADERS ARE CONSISTENTLY PROFITABLE

Good traders need confidence; they need discipline; and the confidence to rigidly stick to their discipline.

—TOM R. PETERSON

Why risk everything on one trade? Why not make your life a pursuit of happiness rather than pain? I decided that I had to learn discipline and money management.

—PAUL TUDOR JONES

YOU MUST DEVELOP a great deal of discipline in order to excel at any endeavor. Without discipline you are on a sailboat without a rudder to steer by. You must have the discipline to do the research to develop a unique trading methodology. Discipline will allow you to test your new trading methodology in real time, using a small percentage of your available funds instead of all your funds. With discipline you will always trade according to your trading rules. Without discipline you will be unable to master your ego, create empowering beliefs, have faith, and develop confidence in your abilities. The lack of discipline will prevent your skill as a trader from progressing.

Everyone knows what discipline is, yet few look forward to undergoing the training and mental exercise needed to develop a highly disciplined trading methodology. You must develop rules that you always apply throughout the rigors of trading. The market will present adversity and prosperity to you; through it all you must maintain the discipline that your trading rules and methodology demand.

Discipline is when you behave according to a set of rules (beliefs). Discipline improves reaction speed, enhances personal abilities, and allows courage to spring forth. Discipline also lends a state of order to what in many cases was chaos. Most people become disciplined by performing a task repeatedly.

Discipline occurs when you take the time to learn new references, and erect a set of rules that you will obey at all cost (convictions). After you construct these rules (which in many cases took considerable time), you will rarely think about how long it took to obtain them when you must behave in a disciplined manner. Discipline dramatically increases the speed in which a particular task is accomplished. This is because there is no internal debate or doubt. Again, using a driving example, you are exercising discipline every time you drive. You have the discipline to obey the rules and follow the safe driving habits that you have learned by repeated experience and training. You react to different driving situations without hesitation. Think back to how you learned your driving discipline, even in situations that at the time may have seemed unnatural. When most of us first learned to drive in the snow, we had been driving for only a short while, and it was a new experience. We were taught that if the car went into a skid, the correct response was to turn the steering wheel into the direction of the skid. When we first heard this, our natural response was "Why?" We thought it was not logical—the wrong response. However, by sliding around in a snow-covered parking lot, we learned that turning into a skid was indeed the correct response. By repetition, in a nonlife-threatening environment, we developed the discipline (belief or rule) to always steer into a skid. Today, if we go into a skid, we do the right thing without even thinking about it! Our belief (or rule) about turning into the skid may have saved our lives many times. In this sense, discipline is nothing more than a belief that is never questioned once it is learned and that we must always obey.

As a trader, you must develop the same level of discipline. In a game where there are no rules that you must follow, you must establish your own rules. The trading environment has no rules telling you when to enter, when to exit, or how many contracts to trade in. The only outside rules are those imposed by your brokerage firm. The brokerage company does not care one iota if you win or lose; it gets a commission regardless. The Commodity Futures Trading Commission (CFTC) and the National Futures Association (NFA) don't care if you make or lose money, provided you obey the reporting and margin requirements.

One of the challenging things about trading is that there are no real rules. There are plenty of general rules, such as "Buy low, sell high." Of course, buying low is never defined. How do you know a price is low? How do you know that it isn't going lower? What exactly is selling high? If you were fortunate enough to buy "low," how do you know that you are exiting the trade at a "high" price? What happens if you exit the trade and the price moves higher? What happens if you indeed do buy at a low price and then exit at a higher price, and after the price drops a little it reverses, continuing much higher? Do you have the rules to reenter the trade? Or do you sit on the sidelines silently fuming that you got out too early?

Here is another perfectly sound general rule: "Let your profits run, and cut your losses short." This is a valid rule, and it is totally worthless. Can you define profit? Is it a 3-point profit? Or is it a 300-point profit? How about a loss? Is it a 3-point or a 300-point move? What does it really mean to let your profits run and cut your losses short? How do you know when you are *in the trade* that your profits are running, and your stop loss point is being kept close? Are the experts who state this rule with solemn dignity implying some sort of ratio? Perhaps that for every possible $100 gain we should be willing to lose $30? Then again, how do we know what ratio to use? How do we know that the losing trade isn't about to turn around and become highly profitable?

One more example: "A market will usually retrace 50 percent of its move." Says who? The "experts" tell us that the markets like to retrace to a Fibonacci number. There are plenty of examples of this taking place, so after we miss a major market move, should we then wait for the 50 percent retracement? What happens if we buy at the 50 percent retracement level, and the market after a brief rally decides to retest down to the 63 percent retirement level? Do we remain long? If so, what about cutting our losses short? What happens if the market retraces 100 percent of its up move? Do we jump in while listening to another general rule that possible double bottoms are good places to go long?

The point I am attempting to make is that there are a lot of general rules, all perfectly valid, about the market at specific times. You must have the discipline to obey your rules every single time without fail.

You must decide what your rules will be.

Using another example, let us say that you decide that you will buy a double bottom. You decide to do so after examining hundreds of charts and literally reviewing hundreds of examples of where the strategy worked. So you patiently wait for the market to fall to a lower level than its previous bottom. Then you watch how the market rallies up before faltering, and subsequently starts dropping toward the previous low. Now, for example's sake, you have decided that you will go long when the price is within 1 percent of the previous low price, and your stop will be 2 percent below the previous low price. Well lo and behold your order gets filled, and sure enough the market bounces up. How do you think you are feeling? Are you feeling good because you are in profit or are you feeling good because you obeyed your discipline? After the initial bounce the market falters, and then drops below the previous low, enough so that you get stopped out. Now how are you feeling? Are you upset that you got stopped out? Are you happy that you got stopped out? Are you happy because you followed your discipline?

Now let us say the market continues to plummet. Are you happy that you got stopped out, thereby avoiding a much larger loss? Are you now happy that you followed your discipline? Or are you mad that you didn't reverse and go short, recouping your long loss and possibly making a small fortune? Are you upset that you went long because obviously (now) it wasn't a valid double bottom? For the sake of argument, let us say that the market, after stopping you out, proceeds lower. Since this new low starts the possibility of a new double bottom, you decide to wait for a small rally, the failure of that rally, and a retest of the lows—so you can get long. Unfortunately for you, when the price rallies it does so sharply, falters just a little, never even comes close to making a double bottom (to fill your standing order), and then proceeds to make life of contract highs! Because you had been stopped out previously, and you didn't go long (since the market didn't make a double bottom), you missed the entire move up. At this point how do you feel? Are you glad that you had the discipline not to enter a market that failed to make a valid double bottom using your rules? If you are upset, what are you more upset with—the market's failure to make a double bottom or your failure to go long?

Proceeding along these lines, let us say that after putting the pain of losing your money behind you, you begin waiting for another possible second bottom. Soon a double bottom comes along in a different market, and following your discipline you go long using the same rules as before. Once again the strategy fails and you lose money. What are you thinking now? Let me ask you a question: How many times do you honestly think that you will repeatedly obey your discipline before abandoning it? The answer for most traders is three or four times. After the fourth loss, they will begin tinkering with their rules and lose the original discipline they had.

Invariably what happens is that after they abandon the discipline they initially had, a trade comes along that works just like they thought it would. How do you think you will feel if, after losing four times in a possible double-bottom trade, you decide to pass on the fifth trade, and it works so well that you would have recovered all your previous four losses and even made a nice profit? All too typically the feeling that most traders get is intense anger, and resentment toward the market and their own shortcomings.

Trading is the most difficult profession you could possibly decide to enter. It is also the most intellectually satisfying. It appears very easy—what could be easier than going long on a double bottom and going short on a head-and-shoulders violation? After all, to be a great success all you have to do is go out and buy a computer program that will identify possible chart patterns, and do what it tells you to do—right?

As in any sport, the real game is played out in the space between your ears. Mastery of trading demands that you take charge of your internal representations, values, and beliefs. Discipline is one of the cornerstones of mastery. Without discipline you will be switching trading programs, methodologies, and newsletters faster than Superman can change into his cape!

How do you become a highly disciplined trader? The answer is similar to mastering your ego, creating faith, and gaining confidence. You must acknowledge how crucial discipline is for your ultimate success. Once you acknowledge its importance, you need to be firmly in charge of your ego, have unshakable faith that the outcome you desire will be accomplished, and the confidence that *your* methodology will work. Then you start the process of changing or creating the necessary beliefs that will empower you to become a highly disciplined trader.

Every parent knows that a baby must first crawl, then walk, and finally run. There are a lot of intermediate stages on that journey. You as a trader must acknowledge that the journey that you are embarking on has land mines everywhere that could halt your progress. Like a baby learning to run, you must start with small steps. You must first determine what beliefs and values you need to succeed. You must research the methodology you believe that you will be most comfortable with; then you must customize it to your individuality. After creating this methodology, you will have to test it on old data to determine if it is valid. Next you must test it in real time, then you must use it with discipline. As you repeatedly test your methodology and your beliefs, you are also creating beliefs and rules about discipline.

The amazing thing here is that it is impossible to have discipline in trading without becoming more disciplined in your personal life. Likewise, it is impossible to have discipline while trading if your personal life is in shambles. Highly successful people are extremely disciplined in their professional and personal lives. Of course there are highly disciplined professionals who have very little order in their personal lives. However, these individuals would be even more successful if they exercised greater discipline in their personal affairs.

The fastest way to become a highly disciplined trader is to realize that discipline is nothing more than a state of consciousness with associated rules. Since these rules are actually beliefs, you can change your existing beliefs about discipline by using the techniques previously mentioned. When you do so, you can actually improve your level of discipline. The rules (beliefs) that you use to determine if you are exercising discipline can be created so they empower you as a trader. When you create rules for being disciplined, you must make them easy to accomplish (true for value rules). If you have too many rules to determine if you are trading in a disciplined way, you will wind up trading with no discipline. This is because you are making discipline too difficult to accomplish.

As you know, rules have high emotional content and a lot of certainty. They're absolute, and we become highly upset if our rules are questioned. However, a rule is a belief, and if we are aware that our existing beliefs about discipline may be lacking, we can change or improve them. The dilemma that beginning traders face in devising new beliefs is that they lack experience (references). This is easy enough to resolve with role models. By asking intelligent questions, we can determine what references our role models use regarding discipline.

Discipline is the ability to consistently follow rules and procedures that have been developed through practice, research, and training in all areas of life. As in everything, if you start taking small steps, before long you will be taking large strides. Discipline also allows you to control how you represent the events that occur in your life. Discipline improves your perceptions while trading. Discipline allows you to disengage, to ignore your ego and emotions, so that you can see the market accurately. Discipline is a virtue and as such it thrives when its importance is acknowledged and encouraged. A trader with discipline is able to maintain her equilibrium when the markets are so choppy that most traders are being badly chopped up. As your level of discipline increases, the amount of control you have over your ego, your level of faith, and your confidence will all begin increasing as well.

The most difficult concept a trader must acknowledge is that the markets are not predictable in an absolute sense. A market can drop in price all the way to zero, and go up to infinity. You need to realize that when you are looking at a chart and deciding that it could be a particular pattern (a double bottom in our example), you are basing that observation on *past* price history. When you are trading, you must be focused only on the instant of time that you are trading in. In other words, if you are day-trading on a five-minute bar chart, you must be totally focused on what the market is doing right now on the five-minute chart. You don't care one iota what it did five days ago—whether it made a high or low. Always ask yourself what the market is doing right now. What is the continuity of thought right now, in this instant of time? Staying in the moment requires a great deal of discipline.

Discipline is the third virtue of trading. Before you can begin to have discipline you must have begun to master the other two virtues—faith and confidence—and to master your ego. As your natural ability progresses, your discipline must be based on solid beliefs. A lot of the internal pain, frustration, and anger can be removed by acknowledging that you are a disciplined trader, and that the markets are totally undisciplined and unpredictable.

6

COURAGEOUS TRADERS WIN BIG

The greatest test of courage on the earth is to bear defeat without losing heart.

—R. G. INGERSOLL

Being a successful trader also takes courage: the courage to try, the courage to fail, the courage to succeed, and the courage to keep on going when the going gets tough.

—MICHAEL MARCUS

COMMON TO THE belief about courage in every culture is the firm resistance to pain, danger, or difficulty. Courage means dealing with the threat of loss of life, liberty, and property by accepting and dealing with fear. It is a very strong virtue, and is a positive character trait in all cultures. Courage allows us to still act reasonably in the face of fear. Courage is not dealing with the threat in the absence of fear. Courage is an emotion and has the power to affect bodily changes. In all cultures courage is a highly valued virtue. It is a strong virtue, and its antithesis is fear—a very strong vice. Since there is a never-ending battle between virtue and vices, courage and fear are engaged in an ongoing contest over which force is more powerful.

Courage can take on as many forms as the variety of the objects that inspired the fear. The courageous person has conquered fear; the coward is overcome by it. Courage implies knowledge of reasonable and unreasonable fears. It is courage that allows us to remain firm when confronted with difficult choices. People who are ignorant or out of control are incapable of courage, even though their actions may be daring.

Courage is related to the emotion of hope. It is through hope that we boldly attack and attempt to overcome the threat. Mental ability, bodily strength, previous experience, loyal friends, and even divine assistance are some of the things that make victory possible. Success or conquest strengthens hope and leads to courage. Courage is also related to what we love and value most. It is when our loves are threatened—life, family, money, possessions, country, and religious beliefs—that our courage is aroused and strengthened. Traders constantly have their loves threatened by the market. Traders obtain victory through their mental abilities, previous experiences (reference), empowering beliefs, and perhaps even divine assistance.

Courage in and by itself is neither moral nor immoral. However, since in many cases the emotion of courage involves the virtue of fortitude, courage is moral. Fortitude is the boundary line between cowardice, which holds us back by fears that reason tells us could be overcome, and rashness, which is a reckless disregard for what should reasonably be feared. Courage is involved in the virtues that are part of fortitude—magnanimity, magnificence, patience, and perseverance. Those who lack courage have given in to a false belief in what true courage is. Many cowardly people will also have the following vices: rashness, presumption, egotistical ambition, vanity, pusillanimity, meanness, and stubbornness.

The difficult choices of trading (or life) demand courage, especially when one outcome seems to preserve our equity, beliefs, and integrity while the other outcome holds financial ruin, despair, being wrong, scorn and mockery, loss of friendship, ridicule, and even temporary ostracism.

Fortitude is a virtue that strengthens courage. Fortitude is a general and a specific virtue. As a general virtue, it must be firm and not readily subject to change. As a specific virtue, it gives the spirit firmness by controlling impulses from the conscious and unconscious mind. When you are confronted with a situation that requires courage, your spirit must remain firm so as to balance the fearful impulse and the foolhardy impulse. The virtue of fortitude strengthens courage against the passion of fear and curbs the immoderate stirrings of foolish daring. Opposed to fortitude are the vices of cowardice and foolhardiness.

Endurance is the more difficult aspect of fortitude, and requires more courage, other things being equal. In attacking an evil object, we at least have some hope that we will overcome it, and hope that we will prove stronger than the threat. In endurance we submit to an evil that seems stronger than ourselves. Attacking an object in the face of danger usually occurs over a brief period of time, whereas endurance usually covers a long, continuous period of time. Endurance in this context is not a mere passive submission to danger and suffering; it involves, more importantly, a strong action of the soul holding steadfastly to the good and refusing to yield to fear and pain.

Successful traders submit their will to the stronger will and dangers of the marketplace. In doing so, they are able to maintain their strength and resolve by the validity of their beliefs. Courage often is described as the ability of the mind to overcome fear. The greatest fear that any individual has is the loss of life. It is for this reason that when most people think of courage they think of a soldier or a martyr. Throughout history people have thought of courage in terms of a battle or of religious persecution. Every culture and religion has its generals, and its martyrs. People think of a great trader as possessing great courage because they *perceive* the trader as risking financial ruin by trading.

In most instances, courage is thought of in relation to fear. Most people do not consider that overcoming anxiety also requires courage. Anxiety and fear both originate from the same part of our psyche; however, they are not the same. Fear originates from a definite source, allowing our conscious mind to focus upon it. This means that fear can be faced, analyzed, attacked, and defeated. In acting upon fear, we participate in it. Courage can act upon fear because fear is an object, and therefore can be engaged. By contrast, anxiety cannot be engaged, since it has no object—our conscious mind is unable to focus upon it.

Fear and anxiety are different, but not separate. They exist within each other. Fear is being afraid of something—a threat, a pain, the rejection or loss of something or somebody, the moment of dying. Anxiety is anticipating the threat, and the resultant possible implications. It is not the negativity itself of the threat that is frightening, but what we perceive it to mean. Our minds will always attempt to turn anxiety into fear, because fear can be met by courage.

Courage is most often associated with combat. The battlefront is where humanity has been trained to look for and discover courage. Some traders equate trading with a constant ongoing battle, and expect to find courage. The courage to trade within your rules requires the fortitude to do what is right, no matter how uncomfortable you feel and no matter what your ego is telling you. Although the courage of an outstanding trader in the marketplace is not as dramatically evident as that of a warrior on the field of battle, it is no less exemplary. In many ways the Samurai warriors of Japan had many of the same beliefs as great traders today.

Traders always face a market that requires them to enter or exit when their emotions tell them to do otherwise. Courageous trading is a crucial element of your success. Possessing courage requires that you accept the responsibility for your profitable trades as well as the losing ones. It is far easier to say that the markets conspired to take your money away from you than it is to accept responsibility for the risk of trading.

You need to understand that even though you possess courage, you will still experience fear. Fear is a natural human emotion, and all traders experience it. It doesn't matter how much experience you have or don't have; everyone will get a visit from Mr. Fear. Outstanding traders will face it, get control of themselves, and obey the rules they developed; cowardly and novice traders will embrace the fear and fail to properly execute their trades.

When do you need courage? The natural answer is when you are fearful. However, do you think that courage might also be required to exit a winning trade? What vice would a trader with a "profitable trade" experience that would create fear? Courage will combat the greed that a trader with a winning trade experiences.

Courage will always counteract the power of fear. Fear results from thinking a multitude of different thoughts. Some of these thoughts are that the market will take your money, that you are leaving money on the table, that the pit just loves to run your stop, or that you have rotten luck. The way I like to see fear is that it is *false evidence* that *appears real,* and that by changing my perspective and trusting myself, there is nothing to be anxious about. Courage is the ability to do the right thing when you are naturally afraid to take action. To understand the virtue of courage then we need to understand the vice of fear, and how it works.

Before you can start to experience the feeling of fear, several things must first take place in your mind. In order to feel fear, you must either be remembering a similar event *in your past* that resulted in pain or you must be anticipating how much this current event might hurt *in the future.* In other words, for your brain to experience the emotion of fear, your mind must be reliving an event in the past or anticipating an event in the future. In both cases mentally you are not in the present moment. Consequently it is impossible for you to see the market as it is.

Once your brain reenters the present moment, it is incapable of experiencing fear. This is because it must make decisions, and is too busy to be anywhere except in the present. Do you remember an event that you were dreading, but then the fear disappeared when it came for you to take action? For some of us it was combat in a war; for others it was making a public speech for the first time. Others may have been totally scared when asking their spouse to marry; still others may have dreaded some sort of examination. The point is that the day before the event we were all scared and afraid, because of our fear. However, when we had to go into action our fear miraculously disappeared.

What happened? Very simply our conscious mind was too busy taking care of the present moment to worry about what might happen in the future, or what happened in the past. The courage that we used to overcome the frightening events of the past is also vitally important to us as traders today. In fact, it is even more important to us as traders, because in most cases we are the only ones who know when our trading methodology indicates that we should enter, exit, or wait for a trade. If we fail to follow the trading methodology that we so laboriously researched, only we will know that our courage was not enough to overcome our fear. There is no audience to judge our courage or lack thereof while trading.

Let me ask you another question: What do you think most traders are afraid of? Many of you will say being wrong and losing money, or leaving money on the table. Some of you will also say that the real issue is that most traders are afraid of being emotionally or financially hurt by the market. I suspect that the core fear of most traders is that they are afraid of themselves!

At the root of all fear is that the trader may do something that results in a lot of pain. The vast majority of traders do not trust themselves to make valid decisions. It is far easier to purchase the advice of others than to do the work necessary to devise their own methodology. The other major reason traders purchase the opinions of others is that when the trade fails to generate a profit, they can blame the loss on someone else, thereby avoiding responsibility for the trade. This is one of the reasons there is such a huge market for trading programs and advisory services. What happens when the trading program fails to make a profit, or the advisory service writer gets the market direction wrong? The trader blames the vendor for the lousy trade! What happens if the trader decides to ignore the "advice of others," trades on his or her own thoughts, and then has a losing trade? Yep, the trader blames the market. What happens when the fill comes back, and it is different from expected? "Well, the pit took my money" is the most common response.

It is very easy to shift the blame to someone else; it is very difficult for most traders to accept responsibility for their own trades. It is even more difficult for traders to trust their own analysis and their decision to enter or exit the market. Why do you think the average trader finds it so hard to have the courage to trust his or her own actions? Because most traders base their decisions on an arbitrary trading methodology that they have no real faith in. The average trader still thinks that there is a holy grail that can somehow be bought.

When you have courage, you will be able to execute your trades with no fear or hesitation. When you have courage, you will be able to focus in the present moment, eliminating the fear of possible loss. You will also be able to trust your own analysis and actions.

How do you develop the increasing levels of courage to faithfully execute your trades? As you should know by now, courage is an emotional state that everyone values. Consequently our level of courage can be increased by changing or creating beliefs that affect courage and fortitude, using the techniques already mentioned. Since courage is something we value, it is controlled by the rules that we attach to it. In order to change or create empowering beliefs, we have to use empowering references. As we increase the amount of discipline we have while trading, we also increase the amount of courage available to us. By strengthening our virtues and starving our vices in order to develop an effective strategy that encompasses our own trading methodology, we will increase the amount of courage we experience.

Traders who have courage accept their fear as being false evidence that appears real. They accept that they could lose their assets. Implied in this acceptance is that they are well aware of when the risk they are exposing themselves to is acceptable or unacceptable. When traders act from a position of courage, they are behaving in accordance with their beliefs without fear—much like a samurai warrior.

The reason the samurai warrior was so feared was that he had the courage to accept his own death, confidence in his abilities, and discipline to overcome his fear. In a lot of ways a highly successful trader today is like a samurai. Successful traders have to accept all the risk of trading, have total confidence in their abilities, and have the discipline to always overcome their fear.

How often do you think that some of the outstanding traders experience fear? How do you think they overcome this fear? Courage will always annihilate fear. The way you can increase your level of courage is by realizing how vitally critical it is to your ultimate success. The next time you start to become fearful, realize that to control fear you must have the courage to focus on the present moment.

Courage is the fourth virtue that all excellent traders possess. All highly effective and successful people use courage in their personal and professional lives. You must have the courage to trust yourself to enter or exit a trade, to make mistakes, to control your ego, and to generate the faith that your outcome will be as you desire. Courage will fortify your confidence, and courage will give you the discipline to master your internal representations of the marketplace.

INTUITION DOESN'T MEAN "INTO WISHING"

Just as one might have to turn the whole body round in order that the eyes should see the light instead of darkness, so the entire soul must be turned away from this changing world until its eye can bear to contemplate reality.

—PLATO

A skilled operator in any field acquires an almost instinctive "feel" which enables him to sense many things even without being able to explain them.

—BERNARD BARUCH

The really valuable thing is intuition. There are no logical paths to these laws, only intuition resting on sympathetic understanding of experience can reach them.

—ALBERT EINSTEIN

INTUITION IS A sublime virtue that a lot of traders have false beliefs about. All beginning traders confuse intuition with "into wishing." It is extremely easy for the novice trader to listen to the thoughts and desires of the unconscious mind, and enter or exit a trade because of "gut feel." However, every outstanding trader possesses intuition and uses it on a daily basis. Even the great system traders who are totally mechanical use intuition in developing their computer-based trading methodologies.

However, many traders confuse an impulsive or irrational thought that originates in their unconscious mind with a valid intuitive thought—after all, intuition is a spontaneous thought originating in the unconscious. The ability to differentiate between the two is often sublime and illusive. Your unconscious mind is always seeking excitement and action, and is very effective at convincing you that you have a really strong intuitive feeling about what the market is about to do. I cannot stress strongly enough that all new traders should ignore any and all intuitive (gut) feelings about trading the market. The only intuitive thoughts that a new trader should act upon are those they can use to develop a methodology.

If you are just starting out, write down all your intuitive thoughts concerning the market in your trading journal. Continue to write your intuitive thoughts on the market for the next 12 months (at a minimum). After several months, start reviewing your journal so you can begin to generate your references about the quality of your intuition. You will begin to see how well your intuitive thoughts and feelings perform. Then after you have worked at increasing your virtues and creating empowering beliefs and are consistently making money over the next 12 months, come back to this chapter and reread it. New traders should use their intuition to develop their trading methodology, not to enter into or exit a trade. Believe me, your bank account will be happy that you did!

Intuition is a very important part of every trader's life. It is what allows you to grasp a concept and implement the concept without understanding all the underlying principles. It is what allows you to recognize a certain behavior of the market even before all the characteristics of that behavior become obvious to your conscious mind. Intuition is what allows you to override your methodology once in a blue moon, thereby increasing your profit or avoiding a loss. Intuition is what allows you to have the breakthrough in designing your trading methodology and, consequently, dramatically increasing its profitability.

In a book written by Jack D. Schwager, Ed Seykota summed up the danger of intuition perfectly: It is very, very easy to confuse intuition with "into wishing." Your beliefs about yourself, unless controlled, will always want to make you believe that you are the most perceptive trader who ever existed. If your unconscious mind can convince your conscious mind to take action, then it will feel wonderful. Your unconscious mind will forget the dozens of losers those "gut hunches" generated (blaming it on other factors), and will remember the one or two winners.

So what exactly is intuition, and how can we become more intuitive? Intuition is increasingly recognized as a natural mental faculty. Intuition is a key element in discovery and problem solving. With the rise of computer power available to the general population, and to traders in particular, the belief that logical arguments and rational programs can be developed to win at the trading game is almost universal. All the books, seminars, and computer programs have so skewed the thinking of most traders that they believe the only possible way to generate consistent profits is by a rational, logical, and sensible trading methodology.

Psychological studies tell us that everything we perceive is an interpretive act. Our perception is influenced by our expectations, beliefs, and values. This is why one trader will say that sugar is in a bear market, and another trader looking at the same exact chart will say that the overall trend is bullish, and that it is only in a correction! For some of the great traders, intuition has done wonders. If reason and empirical observation have set the agenda for trading, and the trader's passion has provided the fuel to do the reasoning, then it is intuition that provides the creative spark of genius.

In the trading universe there are two types of outstanding traders. One type will build up a trading methodology slowly with painstakingly researched facts, much like the tiny marine animals build up a coral reef. The other type will also begin building a trading methodology with carefully researched facts. However, at some point these traders will make a leap of intuitive logic that allows them to soar like eagles.

When we hear or read about great traders, we are seeing the public view. We see the profits that they have made for themselves and/or their clients. We are seeing the final result, which is logical and orderly. We would not see all the false starts and dead ends, all the vague hunches that have been tested and sorted out. As a result, we would conclude that our research must be methodical and logical as well. This is a mistake, since it is our imagination and vague, intuitive thoughts that lead to the discovery of a great trading principle!

There is no logical method of obtaining new ideas. Every discovery about the market will contain an *irrational element of creative intuition.* All great problem solvers are able to make advances in their discipline by perceiving the difficulties, knowing which questions to ask, and understanding how to frame the problem in their mind. Intuition helps traders solve the challenge by deciding where to look for the relevant facts, how to test an idea, how to interpret the data, and how to recognize what is important and relevant.

Do you know why Ray Kroc purchased McDonald's despite the advice of his friends? Because he decided to listen to the feeling in his "funnybone." Let me ask you another question: Does the market exist solely in a "material world" that allows it to be measured, quantified, and defined with precision, or could it be something else altogether? Could it exist only as a manifestation of the beliefs of all the traders involved? Stop reading right now, and take the time to think about it before answering.

The way you answer will tell you a lot about your perception of the market, and how your trading methodology will probably evolve. Your answer will also tell you how your ego wants to perceive the market.

The rational-empirical mode of thinking works best when you can control or predict all the variables that affect the subject you are studying, when you can measure, quantify, and define these variables with precision, and when you have complete and timely information. As we covered in the first chapter, there is no holy grail. The trading market represents hundreds of thousands of variables that no one can predict, quantify, or measure with precision. As an aggregate we can to some degree come up with a representation that can measure, quantify, and define the market. However, since it is an aggregate we are unable to predict with 100 percent certainty what will transpire. Consequently this mandates that a trader work in probabilities.

When we attempt to trade using a methodology that is based solely on the rational-empirical mode, we are setting ourselves up for a lot of frustration. What we are attempting to do is apply a science that was designed to deal with the physical world, and extend it to a nonmaterial, nonquantifiable world. When we attempt to trade exclusively on the rational-empirical approach, we will not be able to deal with critical and nonquantifiable considerations such as perceptions of other traders, the prevailing continuity of thought, and the overall market psychology.

The degree to which you are able to penetrate the transcendent and illuminate the sublime aspects of the market will depend on your success in developing your intuitive skill. The trading environment is a reflection of the opinions (beliefs) of all the traders involved. The traders' opinions will cause them to be (1) sitting on the sidelines watching, (2) already committed 100 percent in the market, (3) in the market but waiting to commit more funds, (4) in the market waiting to exit fully, or (5) in the market and waiting to partially exit the market. These traders could have a profit or a loss, and their opinions will reflect this fact.

Since the trading environment is a reflection of the participants' opinions, the trading waters become muddied. Strict reliance on logical and quantifiable arguments will more than likely impede the trader's vision. Intuition gives the trader an edge, leading to better decisions, more creative ideas, and better and deeper insight. Often when traders start to consider how intuition could benefit them, they also have a certain amount of fear. This fear typically is caused by the thought that intuition is the first step toward intellectual anarchy—because it is arbitrary and nonquantifiable. In the case of the novice trader there is solid justification for this fear. Many new traders will use what they think is intuition as an excuse for their failure, and often they are partially correct. This "intuitive thought" was in fact the ego, which attempted to balance disempowering beliefs of the conscious mind against the unconscious desires and thoughts within a mental context that lacked integrity and discipline. Consequently the new trader is convinced that it was a valid intuitive thought when in actuality it was nothing more than an impulsive thought created by the unconscious mind. Intuition will start to work only after traders have mastered their virtues, vices, and the ability to trust themselves to always act in their best interest. This requires mastery of their beliefs.

Outstanding traders will realize that there must be a balance between the intricate and mutually enhancing relationship between intuition and rationality. They will know that they need a sharp discriminatory rational ability, as well as a better level of intuition. In this manner each ability will supplement the other's strengths.

When we think of intuition we typically think that it follows rationality. You will reason, analyze, gather the facts, have an intuitive thought, then analyze and use reason again so as to verify, elaborate, and apply the intuitive thought. This type of intuitive thought is usually categorized as a "Eureka" experience. However, intuition cannot be confined to the "Eureka" type. Often intuition feeds then stimulates your rational thought, causing your rational conscious mind to evaluate what comes from the intuitive thought. Rational and intuitive thought are both parts of your thinking process, originating in different parts of the mind.

Think of how often you have had insufficient information and not enough time to get all the facts, yet by skipping many of the intermediary steps that strict logic would require, you were able to leap to the correct conclusion? Many times when you make that leap, it is intuition that aids you in the reasoning process. The reason that trading is seemingly so difficult is that, despite insufficient information and market parameters that are changing second by second, you attempt to trade according to a strictly rational-empirical mode of thought.

Intuition will help you look in the right direction, and point you in the right direction to begin the reasoning process. Intuition will help you evaluate conclusions that are derived logically. The quality of the intuitive thought that you possess will be determined by your beliefs about validity of intuition in the trading environment. I cannot tell you how to command or implore intuition to arrive. By examining how you feel about intuition you will discover any negative beliefs that may prevent your sense of intuition from working. Low self-esteem, for example, can lead traders to mistrust anything that they think of, especially if it is a hunch. Fear of change, intolerance of uncertainty, a rigid belief structure, a fanatical adherence to rules, and a belief in standardized procedures will impede intuition. People with a good intuitive sense generally have a high level of self-confidence, courage, and discipline. They are also receptive to unpredictable and surprising news.

Confident thoughts and beliefs, based on faith, and conviction that you deserve the *best answer* will galvanize your intuition into action. When you believe that you can successfully trade in an unpredictable, changeable, and ambiguous market, you will be giving your sense of intuition a vote of confidence.

Often intuition comes to us while we are sleeping, and if we can remember it while awakening we possess a beautiful gift. The literature has countless stories about how an inventor, politician, general, or writer woke from a nap or a night's sleep with the solution to a vexing problem.

Many intuitive people practice some form of meditation. Meditation produces several very real physiological responses. These naturally include relaxation, a modification of the frequency of the brain waves, and the brain arriving at a higher level of consciousness.

Another way to increase your level of intuition is to start practicing yoga. The asanas, or postures, are very effective at decreasing tension and quieting the mind. When the asanas are done correctly, they also increase mental alertness. Perhaps my favorite mental exercise is playing GO, the ancient Japanese game of strategy that is superb at developing many empowering beliefs and strategies. There is no other game that even approaches the mental complexity required by GO.

A very important question for all traders is if the intuitive thought they are experiencing is a real intuitive thought or just an impulsive thought being generated by their unconscious mind on the basis of old beliefs. Often if the thought originates from our unconscious mind, and our conscious mind experiences no resistance to the thought, then in all probability it is not an intuitive thought. If the intuitive thought is valid, then our conscious mind will often experience a certain amount of resistance to it. Here are a few questions to ask yourself to determine if an intuitive thought is valid:

1. *Is the intuitive thought generating an uncomfortable feeling?*
    Generally whenever you have a valid intuitive thought, it will generate a certain amount of discomfort. For example, your intuition tells you to cut your losses on a trade, but you resist and put off doing so because you don't want to own up to having made a mistake, and take a loss before hitting your stop loss point.

2. *Are you experiencing any fear of what others will think?*   If the thought really derives from your intuition, it will generally arouse the attention of other people. Since most people are afraid of ridicule or rejection and have a desire to appear sensible and realistic, they will often ignore an intuitive thought, because it creates a certain amount of fear. As you begin to accept your intuitive thoughts as valid, this fear will usually diminish but not totally disappear.

3. *Is your intuitive thought conforming to the generally accepted view?*   The list of scientists whose intuitive ideas were scorned and deemed impossible by their peers is extremely long. What intuition does best is to go beyond what is generally known and believed. Once again this will generate a certain amount of uncomfortable feeling, or fear.

4. *Does your intuitive thought challenge a cherished belief?*   Many intuitive thoughts can be unsettling. This is because you often have a hard time dealing with the abolition of your old belief and the stabilization of the new belief.

5. *Does the intuitive thought not meet all your standards of completeness?*   Many times a valid intuitive thought will not have all the correlated questions answered. The thought fails to meet all your logical requirements. For example, you wake up one morning with the thought that the coffee trade is in trouble, and that your long position should be removed on the open. Yet because you are unable to satisfy all the correlated questions that will justify the intuitive thought, you remain long, and watch as the market plummets!

6. *Does the intuitive thought generate a certain amount of risk?*   Intuitive thoughts about trading often involve risk. Yet, as in the above example, the risk usually comes from failing to recognize

the validity of the thought. If it is from your ego, generally your ego will fail to see the risk; therefore it is not a valid intuitive thought.

7.   *Do you want your intuitive thought to be right?*   Whenever you find yourself wanting to believe your intuitive thought, more often than not your ego is generating the thought. Is it intuition or into wishing?

8.   *Is it an intuitive thought or an impulsive thought?*   Many people think that "spontaneity" is intuition, because they have lost the concept of discipline. Some people in the name of spontaneity refuse to discipline their drives, urges, desires, wishes, and whims. What may seem like intuition is actually reactive or impulsive behavior. When the ego is not disciplined and under control, it will frequently generate impulsive thoughts to get you to undertake an action because it desires action.

9.   *Is it your intuition or a rebellious ego generating the thought?* The desire to walk a different path will cause many traders to cling to an impulsive thought generated by the unconscious mind. The more outrageous the thought is, the more it will be embraced. The intuitive thought, instead of generating a certain amount of discomfort for being so outrageous, will be embraced.

10.   *Is the intuitive thought accepted without verification?*   Many times when you experience an erroneous thought, you will be predisposed to accept the thought without even attempting to verify its validity. People who are predisposed to intellectual laziness often fall prey to false intuitive thoughts.

11.   *Is it an intuitive thought or an emotional thought?*   Traders who are upset with the market often have a strong intuitive thought that the market is about to reverse. Typically this intuitive thought originates from the desire of the ego to get even with the market.

The best way to validate intuition is by remembering the power of an uncontrolled and undisciplined mind with invalid beliefs. If your intuitive thought comes with a strong feeling of certainty, and is a "comfortable" thought, then it is probably not a valid intuitive thought. Self-deception is a notorious deterrent to using your intuition effectively. When you understand the power of your mind, your mental strengths and weaknesses, you will be able to keep your psychological neuroses from preventing your intuitive mind from functioning.

I would like to reiterate that if you are just beginning your trading career, please do not make any trading decisions on the basis of intuitive thoughts—even if they pass muster on the above questions. *Until you have been trading for at least a year, if not several years, ignore all intuitive thoughts concerning entering or exiting the market.*

The only time you as a beginning trader should use an intuitive thought is when you are designing and testing your trading methodology. In this instance it is perfectly acceptable, and in fact is desirable, to use all the intuitive thoughts that you can come up with. In the research phase of designing your methodology, you will begin to have certain intuitive thoughts that should be vigorously pursued. My urge for caution relates only to making a trading decision on the basis of intuition.

Another way for you to increase your level of intuition about the markets is to quickly scan the charts of different markets. This can be accomplished by randomly turning the pages of a chart book, or changing the screens on a computer. By literally flashing the chart in front of you for a few seconds, you will bring your unconscious mind into play, which will encourage your intuition to become mobilized.

Intuition is the fifth virtue that all excellent traders depend upon. An entire book could be devoted to this topic. My purpose here is to caution new traders that most if not all intuitive thoughts about trading are actually impulsive thoughts being generated by their unconscious mind. Invalid intuitive thoughts will continue until the traders begin to change their beliefs. Again, the only intuitive thoughts you should be receptive to as a new trader are those that help you design and test your trading methodology. However, once your belief structure is mastered and you have gained experience, you will find that your intuitive mind generates valid intuitive thoughts about the markets and can help you increase the effectiveness of your trading methodology.

PERSISTENT TRADERS LOVE TO TRADE

What separates the 1% from the other 99% is a lot of hard work. It's perseverance. You have to love to do it.

—TOM BALDWIN

There is nothing which persevering effort and unceasing and diligent care cannot overcome.

—SENECA

Flinch not, neither give up nor despair,
If thou dost not invariably succeed
in acting from right principles.

—MARCUS AURELIUS

PERSISTENCE IS A virtue and a belief about oneself that every individual who has ever excelled in any endeavor has possessed. It is a common word that individuals who have become outstanding at their craft often use to describe how they accomplished their goals in life. They were able to steadfastly continue pursuing their goal, refusing to yield to the opposition. Many traders have lost several fortunes in the pursuit of their ultimate goal. The perseverance they demonstrated is common to all successful people. The ability to pursue a desired outcome with tenacious perseverance is a quality that every highly successful individual has developed.

It is one thing to perform a single act requiring control of your beliefs, confidence, or courage. It is another thing altogether to continue using empowering beliefs, possessing confidence and courage for a prolonged period of time in spite of continued opposition. A mental fatigue tends to overcome your emotions when you must persist in a course of action for a prolonged period of time. When you have persistence, you are able to fortify your beliefs while pursuing a difficult course of action until the desired outcome is accomplished.

Without a firm character trait of persistence, no successful individual would be able to overcome the challenges encountered while in the pursuit of excellence. Without the virtue of perseverance, no outstanding trader would be able to attain the outcome he or she desires. Individuals who are able to remain persistent will be able to overcome cowardice, stubbornness, and other fears.

One challenge posed by persistence is that it is often mistaken for stubbornness (which is a major vice). Stubborn people will not abandon a course of action when they should. Stubborn people will not be receptive to the idea that the present course of action is not working. In order to become outstanding, people must be flexible in their thinking. Isn't it interesting that as people age, their minds as well as their bodies often become more rigid?

All outstanding individuals have mastered the ability to control their mind, maintain faith that they will accomplish their goal, maintain confidence in the face of challenges, adhere to the discipline required, and remain persistent in the pursuit of their outcome—all the while remaining flexible in their tactics and approach. Mentally people need to see that the outcome they are experiencing is not what they desire. Consequently they must have the flexibility to modify their approach until the outcome is aligned with their desires. Delusional individuals continue doing the same thing, all the while thinking that they will get a different outcome. Traders are confronted with a multitude of constantly changing market variables.

The mental willingness to persistently pursue their outcome in spite of seemingly insurmountable challenges will guarantee that eventually the traders will accomplish their goals.

Let me ask you another question: How long do we allow a toddler to persist in the attempt to walk before we stop trying to teach? Naturally we do not place an arbitrary limit on how long it will take the child to learn to walk. Likewise we do not place a time limit on our attempt to teach a child how to speak. Then why is it that so many adults apply themselves in learning a new skill only for some arbitrary length of time? They are happy if they learn what they desire within that arbitrary length of time. All too often however, when they are unsuccessful in learning within that arbitrary period, they simply give up. We all know people who have done this—in many cases, it is ourselves!

Persistence is the ability to continue our present course of action in the face of resistance. There are few things more frustrating in life than attempting to master a new skill and consistently not succeeding. Persistence in the face of adversity is a virtue that all too many people ignore. All famous and successful people achieved their position because they had the ability to persevere. All traders who consistently make profits do so because they learned to persist in the face of adversity until they won.

The ability to possess a tenacious persistence requires well-founded empowering beliefs, a strong feeling of faith, confidence originating from faith but based on abilities, and a well-disciplined mind that promotes a strong feeling of courage, which allows you to trust your intuition.

You can constantly improve your level of persistence in everything by remembering how important it actually is. The critical point to remember is that there is a fine line between persistence and stubbornness. You must constantly be aware of how you can often accomplish your goals more quickly and even more easily by changing your beliefs and strategies. As Anthony Robbins wisely observes: "Everyone I meet knows more than me in a particular area, and I know something more than anybody else in a particular area." As you persistently apply yourself to a given endeavor, always remember that there may be someone who has already figured out an easier way to accomplish what you are striving for.

This is a fairly short chapter; however, it is very important. Every successful trader has a core virtue of persistence. It is a critical virtue. Without the ability to remain persistent in the face of seemingly endless adversity, you will never reach the outcome that you desire.

INTEGRITY — MUCH MORE THAN MERE HONESTY

Let unswerving integrity always be your watchword.

—Bernard Baruch

Integrity without knowledge is weak and useless, and knowledge without integrity is dangerous and dreadful.

—Samuel Johnson

INTEGRITY IS THE ability of a trader to trade with complete and uncompromising adherence to his or her virtues, beliefs, and personal trading methodology. Traders with integrity have the ability to enter into a trade with undivided attention, and are not distracted by what anyone else is saying or doing. This is possible only because the traders have consciously worked on improving their virtues and beliefs, and the quantity and quality of their references. They know that their trading methodology is completely valid.

People who trade from integrity are operating from a position of strength, free of fear, totally in charge of their mental environment. They will rigorously obey the rules they have developed for their trading methodology. Specifically traders with integrity are immune from what their vices, disempowering beliefs, and unconscious are telling them about the rational reasons the market is acting in a certain way. They will continue to trade within their trading methodology. Quite simply, traders with integrity will be brutally honest at all times with themselves. They will always hold themselves responsible for their actions and beliefs, and will demand a strict code of personal conduct.

In order for you to trade from a position of total integrity you must master the following:

- Your ability to control your unconscious thoughts.

- Your ability to create empowering beliefs.

- Your confidence in your abilities.

- The discipline to obey your trading rules at all times.

- The ability to have courage to consistently execute your trading methodology.

- The ability to tell the difference between being "into wishing" and intuition.

- The ability to persistently develop your trading abilities in the face of hardships.

Successful traders with integrity will have integrated all their virtues and trading beliefs into a unified set of principles, and vanquished their vices.

Integrity is the highest possible virtue. The foundation of all virtues is mastering your mental environment, and the pinnacle of virtues is your integrity. All the other virtues are sandwiched between them, and they are all codependent. It is very important for you to master all your character traits so you can accomplish your goal of being a successful trader. It is also easy to understand why there are very few books that address the virtues a successful trader needs. It is a fairly easy matter to educate a person on how the moving averages, stochastic, relative strength index (RSI), candlesticks, and cycles behave. It is more difficult to teach a trader the more esoteric applications of the RSI, Gann Analysis, Elliott Wave, and other esoteric mathematical studies. However, it is an entirely different matter to tell new traders that the biggest obstacle to becoming excellent traders is their own beliefs and values. All the various analyses or trading techniques are an attempt to put the market action into a "picture" or "representation" that the trader can then internalize and profit from. While it is difficult to master the inner workings of the RSI, it is even more difficult to master one's virtues, vices, and beliefs.

New traders, and society as a whole, want to believe that by spending money on a problem it may be eliminated easily with little or no effort. Do you think most traders want to spend the time and effort to validate Elliott Wave theory to their conscious and unconscious mind when they can buy a program that will analyze the market from the Elliott Wave perspective and tell them the exact moment they should enter their order? When traders "pay their dues" and perform the research, investing the time to master a particular technique, they will internalize that technique into their psyche. They are then in a unique position to use their unconscious and conscious mind to master the technique, with intuition available to help them modify the technique. When you first heard the story of how a child told the world that the emperor had no clothes on, did you stop to ask yourself why it took a little child to recognize the truth? The answer was that there was no adult with integrity present. Integrity is not something that many people have in today's society.

I really want to avoid getting into a philosophical argument; however, to have integrity, you must adhere to certain absolute moral norms. The two universal moral norms are "Love God above all else" and "Love thy neighbor as thyself." These two universal norms are what will strengthen all your virtues, and help you annihilate your vices.

Every individual who has succeeded on a massive scale has a tremendous sense of integrity. If you were to ask such people if being honest is the same as having integrity, they would tell you that there is a huge difference between the two. Just about everybody confuses honesty with integrity, since in today's world these words are often used interchangeably. Honest people are truthful and credible with others and themselves. People with integrity have an uncompromising adherence to their beliefs—a trait that transcends honesty. A person of religious faith would say that such people are in an unimpaired spiritual state.

Integrity derives from the word "integrate." People with integrity have unified all their virtues and beliefs into a harmonious whole that is larger than the sum of the individual virtues. A synergistic energy is created as an individual begins to master his or her virtues. As these virtues come together, they begin to annihilate the vices. Consequently a trader with integrity will possess a spirit that is indomitable. While most people are honest, few possess integrity in the full sense of the word.

It may appear that there is a subtle difference between honesty and integrity; let me assure you that there is a huge difference. Do you think that an honest person could lack faith, have no confidence, be a coward, have the discipline of a jellyfish, and possess no intuition? Without a doubt honesty is a virtue that all traders must possess. *Integrity is the summation of all the virtues.* People with integrity will hold themselves to a higher standard than just being honest. Integrity requires mastering and integrating all the virtues and beliefs we have been discussing. A trader can possess some of the desired character traits and have no integrity. Yet a trader with integrity will possess all the virtues, many of which are not mentioned in this book.

In order to become an excellent trader, you will need to have total integrity. You must always be able to know exactly why you entered or exited a position. You must be brutally honest with yourself on what your motivations were. As you hold yourself to a much higher standard than any one else ever could, you will transform!

You must make possessing integrity while trading, and integrity in your entire life, of utmost importance. If you achieve integrity, few will be able to surpass you.

10

FLEXIBLE TRADERS ADAPT AS THE MARKETS CHANGE

Human nature makes traders hopeful when they should be fearful. When traders have losses they become hopeful, and when they have profits they become fearful. The net result is small profits and large losses.

—JERRY RAFFERTY

THE VAST MAJORITY of novice traders have never taken the time to consider how important flexibility is to their success, or the success of the professional trader. The amazing thing is that most successful traders have many beliefs that require them to be disciplined, and to be flexible. Beliefs about flexibility will also be found among outstanding athletes, businesspeople, and other individuals who have succeeded on a massive scale.

Flexibility originates with the unconscious realization at an early age that without flexibility we may not reach our immediate goal. As we get older we realize consciously and unconsciously how important flexibility is to all animals, plants, and other people. One of the laws of nature is that in order to survive, every living thing must be flexible to some to degree or another. Every living plant is flexible—some more than others. In many cases the more flexible the plant is, the faster it will grow. Evidence of this is everywhere you look. For example, a poplar tree is much more flexible than an oak tree. Guess which one grows faster? Also, which one do you think will survive a hurricane in better condition? In case you didn't know, a poplar tree grows so fast that many people consider it an oversize weed! Isn't evolution nature's way to exhibit its ability to be flexible?

Flexibility is the ability to adapt our approach either mentally or physically to a problem so that we can overcome it and still get our desired outcome. Anyone who has ever walked along a barbed wire fence can remember seeing how any tree used as a fencepost grew around the barbed wire. The tree desired to grow, but the wire was hindering its growth. So the tree, while retaining its nature of being a tree, simply "flexed" or bent itself around the wire. Similarly traders will have constant problems that require the ability to be flexible while remaining disciplined and true to their own beliefs. Do you believe that a disciplined trader is a rigid trader? What do you imagine Jimmy Rogers would say about discipline and flexibility?

Thinking in a flexible way is the ability to perceive a different approach to the problem, so that we may still accomplish the desired outcome. Our ability to grow (or learn) from the challenge allows us to more easily handle similar problems in the future. As we increase our problem-solving abilities, we become more flexible. In other words, when we are mentally flexible enough so that we can overcome a new problem in a new way, we are creating new references that will affect our beliefs about ourselves and the problem. When people are able to "bend" their thinking around a new problem without losing sight of their desired outcome, they have the ability to remain in the moment and to keep their beliefs intact.

We first learned the concept of flexibility when we were children. One of the first instances I can remember of my children exhibiting flexibility was when we ran out of their favorite ice cream, and the only ice cream left in the freezer was my favorite. The desired outcome they wanted was to eat ice cream, so they adapted their beliefs about ice cream, deciding that my flavor would be acceptable. Likewise, a commodity trader will have to be flexible in all aspects of trading in order to be successful. This could be something as obvious and mundane as having a satellite feed go down immediately after placing a trade order, requiring the trader to implement or quickly obtain a backup plan. However, it also could be something more difficult such as having to adopt a new perception of the market when it become obvious that the trader's current perception is erroneous. This could occur, for example, immediately after the trader establishes a long position based upon a five-minute chart, and the market begins to drop.

Another example is a trader who uses a certain methodology to determine the trend, then waits for a bullish divergence in the RSI, buying on the open the next day. If the trader's rules for defining a bullish divergence were very rigid, there would be a good chance of missing the move up move because the market action did not meet all the rules of a perfect divergence. However, with a more flexible approach our trader would be able to accept a less than perfect "divergence," and therefore not miss the move. This is not to say that rigid rules should not be used; however, there is a time and place for rigidity and, most important, a time and place for flexibility. In this case the flexibility would come into play when the trader was defining the rules (beliefs) about what price action would construe a bullish divergence.

All traders will experience new problems that they do not know how to deal with and feel uncomfortable dealing with. However, once they have overcome a particular problem, they develop a feeling of certainty that they can overcome it again. Unfortunately, there seems to be a constant supply of new problems that enter into the trader's life. As the ability to be flexible increases, the ability to resolve new problems also increases. Successful traders know that flexibility improves their perception of the marketplace and also improves how fast they can react to a new market environment. Flexibility allows successful traders to fight their fear because it forces them to be less rigid in their thinking. They know that as the ability to be flexible increases, their level of resourcefulness will be increased. The amazing thing about flexible thinking is that it enables you to perceive alternative methods to accomplish your goals.

As people age, not only does their physical flexibility start to diminish, but their ability to think outside the box as well. Mental flexibility means thinking in such a way that you can bend your mind around the problem and arrive at a new solution without losing sight of your goal, or your values. Although flexibility is not a belief as much as the ability to think in a certain way, it is affected by your beliefs. In order to increase your level of mental flexibility, you need to determine which of your beliefs could empower or disempower your ability to be flexible.

Typically when rigid traders are asked to describe their beliefs (rules) about what it takes before they can experience something they value, they will use a lot of "ands" to link all their beliefs together. Consequently they have a very rigid system of beliefs that must occur before they experience an emotional feeling that they value. For example, if you were to ask rigid traders how they know when they are successful, they might say: "When seven trades out of ten are profitable, and of those seven five of the underlying contracts move at least 5 percent, *and* my broker tells me that I am the best trader she is working with, and none of my trading buddies comes even close to my profitability, *and* the trades work out exactly like my methodology predicted." Another example is asking such traders to describe the methodology for going long. They might say: "I go long only when the 9-period moving average crosses above the 45-period moving average, *and* in the preceding 20 days there was a double bottom, *and* the volume is increasing." In almost all cases the rules (or beliefs) are linked together with "and." The more rules a trader has that are linked together by the word "and," the more rigid the trader becomes. Consequently the more difficult it becomes to accomplish what the trader seeks. The problem with rigidity is that it leads to emotional, physical, or fiscal death. The most rigid people in the world are those who are six feet underground.

I once met a trader who had 59 rules before he would go long. He had done extensive back-testing that verified that in "almost" every case when those 59 rules had been met—it resulted in a profit. Unfortunately the trader blew up his account before he could prove the validity of those rules. Why? Because his rules were so exact that long periods went by before he got a signal; consequently he would lose his discipline, ignore his rules, and go long when he had a gut feel that the market was about to go up. In addition, he had an inherent problem with his 59 rules. In effect, what he had done was to optimize his methodology to such a degree that it almost guaranteed that the next actual signal would be a loser (I know that sounds bizarre). In a later chapter we will examine optimization and why it usually fails. The point right now is that because this trader had 59 rigid rules, he was guaranteeing that he would lose all his money. If he had researched a methodology that perhaps had 9 rules (or beliefs) about the market that were linked together using some "or" instead of just "and," his probability of success would have been higher. However, this approach takes much more insight and work to accomplish.

The mental ability to be flexible in your thinking is a requirement for success as a trader. It may seem that flexibility and discipline are opposed to each other. However, this is not the case. Traders without discipline will behave inconsistently, without conviction, and with no rules. They have little confidence, and little faith that they will accomplish the desired outcome. Disciplined traders will behave consistently, with conviction, confidence, and the knowledge that they will accomplish their final outcome. However, without flexibility their approach to the markets will be very rigid, almost guaranteeing their eventual ruin. The markets are a very fluid, and dynamic entity—just the opposite of rigidity. Consequently a disciplined trader with no flexibility will be constantly frustrated by the action of the markets. This frustration often leads to anger and resentment, which in turn lead to a desire to get even with the market.

Flexible traders, on the other hand, will realize that they are working with a very fluid, dynamic, and flexible entity. They will understand that although they must have discipline, they must also always be able to overcome the problems that the market throws forth. As a very successful trader once said: "You have to know when to follow your rules, and you also have to know when it's time to bend them."

I find that yoga not only helps me be flexible but also simultaneously strengthens my discipline. It is extremely difficult to overcome limiting beliefs about your physical flexibility by practicing yoga, and not let it affect your mental beliefs regarding your mental abilities and the markets. Your ability to be flexible is the result of developing your character traits of persistence, intuition, courage, discipline, and faith. There is a huge difference between a disciplined flexible trader and an undisciplined flexible trader.

Flexible traders are always willing to modify their methodology and beliefs in order to accomplish their goal of consistently producing profits. They are always ready to change their perception if it will increase their performance. As new information enters into the conscious mind, flexible traders will be ready to adapt to it, provided it meets all their correlated beliefs. Their level of discipline remains; in fact, it is because they are disciplined traders that they can be flexible in their perception and approach.

Do you think that Albert Einstein had tremendous mental discipline as well as the ability to be extremely flexible in perceiving new realities? Your responsibility is to develop the mental flexibility to perceive new methodologies and new market realities. What worked in the past may not work so well in the future.

11

FEAR—EVERY-ONE HAS IT; YOU MUST CONTROL IT

It is in the moment of your decision that your destiny is made.

—ANTHONY ROBBINS

I think one of my strengths is that I view anything that has happened up to the present point in time as history. I really don't care about the mistake I made three seconds ago in the market. What I care about is what I am going to do from the next moment on.

—PAUL TUDOR JONES

I prefer not to dwell on past situations. I tend to cut bad trades as soon as possible, forget them, and then move on to new opportunities. After I bury a dead trade, I don't like to dig up the details again.

—ED SEYKOTA

HE DISEMPOWERING BELIEFS and perceptions you possess are typically negative emotions. Negative emotions are what all excellent traders strive to rid themselves of. Up to this point we have been talking about virtues, and empowering beliefs that a successful trader must possess. Now it is time to talk about some of the biggest vices a trader will have to deal with. As discussed previously, our beliefs generate a lot of these negative emotions because our expectations (rules) have not been met. We must overcome the negative beliefs, rules, and references about the markets (and to a large degree about life) that create our negative emotions and encourage our vices. In almost every case a novice trader will experience negative emotions while his or her trading account is creating losses. The primary emotion will be fear, which leads to anger, doubt, indecision, despair, and then resentment.

All highly successful people have mastered the ability to take their negative emotions and use them to motivate themselves. In effect, they have the ability to re-present (present again) the event that led to the negative emotion, and change the negative emotion into a neutral or even positive one. Every event that you experience is remembered by your conscious and unconscious mind regardless of whether you want it to or not. It is then remembered in the future, and re-presented to your conscious and unconscious mind, often creating fear or anger.

If you and your best friend were standing at a corner, and saw an accident where one car veered into the path of another car, you would both tell the police officer a different version of what transpired. You may have been aware of the velocity of the impact, the color of the car, and the sound. Your friend may not have seen any of that because he was focused on the dog that ran into the street, precipitating the accident. As you remember the accident, you will be attaching certain emotional feelings to it. You are *re-presenting* the accident to your mind, with all the emotional feeling you originally associated to it. The reality is that you are seeing only a small part of the overall picture. Now the emotional energy that you attach to the accident could empower you to become a better driver or, negatively, could create limiting beliefs. In other words, you could associate in your mind that you must always wear your seat belt (an empowering belief), or alternatively you could decide never to get a dog because dogs get run over by cars. This is a limiting belief in the sense that you would never know the joy a dog can bring.

Everything we experience through our five senses, all our emotions, and everything we vividly imagine is remembered by our mind. Our unconscious mind is unable to tell the difference between an actual event and an imagined event. When we subsequently remember that event, our conscious or unconscious mind can only re-present the event as it was initially saved to our memory. What we saw is determined by where our focus was. Our focus in turn is determined by our thoughts, which fall under the influence of our beliefs and values. Consequently because of our internal beliefs and values, we are able to perceive, and therefore remember, only a small part of the real event. When we recall an event, we also remember (consciously and unconsciously) all the emotions (actual or imagined) linked to that event. Our sense of reality becomes distorted by our perceptions.

Like eyewitnesses to an accident, novice traders will "experience" the same price movement and yet have different explanations of exactly why the market is behaving the way it is. Every trader sees the price movement through sunglasses that are tinted by personal beliefs and rules, associated emotional feelings, and expectations. No matter how hard the novice tries to see the price movement with clear vision, it remains tinted. Thus a novice trader will usually perceive the price movement with a lot of emotional intensity, whereas a successful trader will re-present the price action in a more detached, objective way.

An important concept to remember is that each of your experiences is remembered in a certain way, with certain emotional attachments, depending on what you were focusing on and the emotional and physiological state you were in at the time. Whenever you remember a given event, your mind will re-present it the way it was stored. The thing to keep in mind is that when you underwent the experience, you actually experienced only a small part of the overall "event." So when you subsequently remember that event, the emotional feelings attached to it are much larger than they should be. In effect, the linked emotional feelings are being overrepresented to your mind.

The primary negative emotion all traders experience is fear. This fear is created by a belief that there is an impending threat or danger to something they hold value in. Traders value many things, such as money, beliefs, expectations, and other values.

So is losing money while trading a bad thing? Just about every trader out there will say "of course." Of course most traders lose all the money they started trading with. Of course it is logical that it is a bad thing to lose money. Of course only a fool wouldn't get upset about losing money!

As you might suspect, this is a loaded question. The truth is that no one wants to lose money. The big difference is that successful traders will experience one set of beliefs and emotions when a trade results in a loss. Novice traders will experience an entirely different set of emotions. The key lies in how the traders represent the loss to themselves. Excellent traders will represent the loss in a manner that empowers their beliefs about the market.

Novice traders will represent the loss in a very negative manner, typically by strengthening their disempowering beliefs and other vices.

When you had a financial loss, what emotions did you experience? Was it anger, disappointment, frustration, fear, resentment, intense anxiety, or relief? Did you experience all of them? Most novice traders will see their loss as confirmation that their trading abilities are not adequate enough to anticipate the market's direction. All traders experience disappointment when their expectations are not fulfilled. Whenever they enter a trade, they will have certain expectations about the outcome. Naturally they will expect to be right about the direction of the market, so that their equity grows. In many cases they will expect that their unique perception of the market will allow them to enter into the trade, and that the market will then follow their lead. They will also expect the market to behave in a certain semilogical manner. As we can see, there are many expectations that a novice trader will have on *one* trade.

People get upset when their expectations are not met. If you expect to make money on entering a trade, then you are setting yourself up for disappointment. The market cannot be predicted with absolute certainty. However, by diligent research you will find a pattern or patterns that you believe work most of the time. So instead of entering into a trade with an expectation that might not be fulfilled, generating disappointment, you want to enter into the trade with an expectation that probably will be fulfilled, generating empowering feelings about yourself. This expectation could be that the market will tell you *after* you enter the trade if you are going to make money based on your observed pattern. With this expectation you will not get upset, since the market will always tell you—that is, your expectation will always be met. A different empowering expectation could be that by entering the trade you will find out if your pattern will work *this time* or not. If it works, you made some money; if it doesn't, then you lost some money. In both cases your focus has changed, and you are in charge.

An expectation is nothing more than a belief that an anticipated event or outcome will come to be. In other words, it is a belief that another belief will be validated. Let's say we have a belief that a trading methodology using a breakout of a point-and-figure chart combined with a dual moving-average crossover is highly profitable. We have a multitude of beliefs here. We have a belief that a point-and-figure chart is a valid way to perceive the market, and another belief that a breakout is significant. We have a belief that dual moving averages have validity, and another belief that when the shorter-term average crosses the longer-term average it is significant. If we then enter a trade based upon that methodology, we will naturally expect a profit. So our belief about the outcome is based upon other beliefs. What happens if our well-tested methodology generates losses when we trade with actual money?

Whenever they are in a trade, great traders realize that their perceptions are being influenced by their position. They have come to realize that they must constantly monitor how they feel, because what is actually happening in the marketplace is different from their perceptions. Great traders know that whenever they start focusing on the monetary value of the trade, instead of the structure of the price movement, they are distorting the market action, and they should be thinking of going flat. They also know that whenever they start saying "I hope—," it is their unconscious mind telling them to exit the trade. They have come to realize that the best way to regain their perspective without undue influence from the market is to go totally flat.

The vast majority of traders react to a loss with negative emotions, typically anger. This is because the market made them wrong, and their beliefs weren't validated. When their methodology indicates another trade, they experience a lot of fear. After talking to literally hundreds of traders about their losses, I discovered that the almost universal comment was "Yeah, the market took my money." The second most likely comment was "The floor ran my stops and stole my money!" In other words, it wasn't their actions that lost their money, but the action of the market. Is it any wonder that the vast majority of traders are fearful of the market? Are you more afraid of the market or of your own actions?

Almost all great traders whom I have studied or talked with have started from a mental framework similar to that of novice traders. Like novice traders, they experienced the emotions of fear and anger at their losses. However, they were able to realize that their perceptions, values, references, and rules had to change. Do you know what made them realize that the way they represented the market had to change? Like great athletes and other outstanding performers, they literally realized at a very distinct moment in time that they had to change their internal beliefs. Often it was when they were experiencing maximum pain, almost more than they could bear.

For many (but not all) great traders, it was a point in time after they had lost everything. They had lost their house, car, furniture, and in some cases their marriage. They had lost all their money to the market. At a singular moment they realized that they had to find a new career or change their beliefs about the market. At this point in time they realized they could continue to blame the market for their problems, or they could accept responsibility for their present predicament. In many cases when they lost everything they realized that they were more than their possessions, and that their trading behavior did not accurately represent who they were. For most, this realization took place at what they called a "black time" or "a pretty bleak time." The experience of losing everything actually liberated their thinking, and they realized how crucially important their internal values were.

In effect, all these future great traders realized (consciously or unconsciously) that they had to *decide* to strengthen their virtues and starve their vices. This is where mastering the nine virtues and beliefs of trading enters into the equation. By mastering all of them, you will be able to triumph over your fears and painful experiences. What are you afraid of while trading? Is it losing money? Is it that the market has the power to absolutely ruin you financially? Is the trading environment your friend or your enemy? Is it a threat that you must deal with? A very important question, when you are looking at the market and thinking of making a trade is: What exactly are you focusing on? Are you focusing on what the market can take away from you? Are you thinking about how much money you might lose or how much money you might make? Are you loving the market or resenting it?

UNDERSTANDING FEAR

I ask these questions in an effort to get you to think about what your beliefs and perceptions are. It is your perceptions that are controlling your outcome in the trading environment. When the price begins to move, do you see it as an opportunity to profit or as a threat, a way to lose money? Do you think the market has only a few "good moves" a year, or do you think the market is in perpetual motion? Successful traders will perceive that the market is in perpetual motion, and that the price movement is an opportunity for them to profit. If you are focusing primarily on how much the market can take away from you, and then secondarily on how much money you might make by entering a particular trade, then you will typically accomplish what you are primarily focusing on—a loss.

Almost all novice traders experience a very common fear—the fear of a loss (a financial loss or a belief loss). This overriding fear derives from the multitude of fears that they possess. The most common one is that they are not able to anticipate the market direction correctly. This assumes that someone else can. Did you ever stop to think that if anyone could accurately predict the market, it would cease to exist? Another fear among novice traders is that they will not act in their best interest. The more they examine the market and attempt to anticipate the market direction—the more analyzing they do—*the more they will exclude other, perhaps vital, information.* These traders also fear that somehow they may actually win, and that they do not deserve to win because they did not "work" for it.

In a desperate attempt to combat their fear, understand the market, and avoid more losses, novice traders will include more variables in their analysis, use more mathematical studies, and obtain more news feeds, thereby focusing even more intently on these additional variables. This practice virtually guarantees that they will overlook other data that could be vitally important. However, no trader can absorb all known facts about a particular market, since there will always be somebody or some news event that will affect the price action unexpectedly. All too often this means that traders will create their losses simply because they focused on trying to avoid a loss. Their unconscious mind helped them get exactly what they were focusing on!

Whenever you make a decision while you are experiencing fear, it will almost always be a wrong decision. For example, if in an effort to reduce your level of fear while trading you decide to add more indicators to your methodology, you will most likely fail to accomplish the desired outcome of consistent profits. This is because your ability to correctly decide what to do while being afraid is greatly diminished by the beliefs that you are currently experiencing.

Successful traders are focused on the markets in an empowering way. They are constantly looking for market information that allows them to profit. They are more concerned with information that reinforces what they want, and they are less concerned with information that reinforces what they fear the most. In other words, their focus is on what they desire—not on what they don't want. It is very difficult for novice traders to change their beliefs without realizing how important the trading virtues are. It seems that every ad that new traders see tells them how easy it is to make money—if they will only buy this new computer program or this overpriced trading course. Generally the more a product is advertised, the more worthless it is. People will always seek out quality. A producer of quality is able to enjoy word-of-mouth advertising, without the expense of a large advertising budget.

Once your fear starts to diminish, you will begin seeing certain market characteristics that you were previously blind to, thereby allowing you to start producing consistent profits. Many traders will refuse to define a loss, insisting that it is only a paper loss, that they are right, and that the market is wrong. This is because their ego is attempting to remain in control, and maintain a false sense of certainty.

So let me ask you a question: What exactly is fear? What has to happen for you to experience fear? How do you know that you are experiencing fear? Which of your needs (if any) is fear meeting?

Remember, as an acronym FEAR stands for *f*alse *e*vidence *a*ppearing *r*eal. What exactly does that mean? Fear is an emotional feeling that your conscious and perhaps unconscious mind is experiencing because it is apprehensive, sensing impending danger to your beliefs, rules, or values. As your mind experiences these feelings, it is remembering the stored-away references that are in some way linked to this current event. The references could be real or imagined; they could be accurately remembered (highly doubtful) or full of misrepresentations. In fact, your references are in all probability more false than true. Remember that your ability to accurately represent the event to your mind is determined by your beliefs. It is your beliefs that are influencing your ability to perceive the event as it is actually unfolding. The more emotionally intense the references, the more likely the event will be represented in your mind in an erroneous manner. Consequently your ability to take action will be adversely affected.

Fear originates because your mind (consciously and/or unconsciously) is undisciplined. The root of the problem is that your current beliefs have allowed fear to grow in your mind until it is almost unmanageable. When you accept the validity of disempowering references and beliefs, you are guaranteeing more fear in the future.

Fear will always give you more rigidity (traders have to possess an open mind), despair, anxiety, doubt, indecision, hesitancy (ever wonder why it is so hard to "pull the trigger"), frustration, anger, and pain. Fear is the reason that 99 percent of all new traders eventually quit their attempt to trade. Fear is an emotional feeling that will cripple anyone in any endeavor. It is an emotion that must be dealt with today, so that it will have less power in the future. There is no way to totally eliminate fear at all times, since it is a normal emotion in every sane individual. People who never experience fear have nothing to value—even life itself. The secret is to control and minimize any fear that arises before trading. You can then trade in a mental and emotional state untinted by fear.

For most of us, fear arises over the possibility of incurring a monetary loss, missing a trade that subsequently becomes a huge winner, prematurely exiting a winning trade and thus missing extra profits, losing self-esteem, feeling shame or embarrassment, being flat-out wrong about the market, or perhaps most importantly losing a valued belief. We fear losing a valued belief because we know that doing so will force us to change. Unfortunately, the majority of traders out there believe that change equals pain. When an existing belief is threatened, we perceive it as actually threatening some of our basic needs. Remember that our conscious, and/or unconscious mind will determine that a belief is valid if it meets some or all of the basic human needs: certainty, variety, significance, and connection.

In other words, if we have slowly developed a belief that the market is about to behave in a certain way, we will be very hesitant to change that belief. The more emotional intensity we have linked to this belief, the more difficult it becomes to change. Opinions if threatened generate a low level of emotional feelings; however, if our conviction is threatened, we will become very protective and will start to get very upset that our conviction is even at issue. Consequently if through a lot of research we have come up with certain beliefs about the market, and we enter into the trade, and it works as expected, we begin to change our belief into a conviction. However, what happens when we enter into a trade that fails, generating a rather large loss? We tend to get angry at the market. What happens if the subsequent trade also fails? We not only become angry that it didn't work, but we also start to experience some fear. Why? Is it because we might lose some more money? Or is it because our belief about the market action is being threatened? In most cases, if we used correct money management rules (most novices utterly fail in this are), our fear is that the belief is not valid. Thus begins a vicious circle of fear, more research, new beliefs, more fear—the black hole of trading.

What is an expectation? Do you remember? It is a belief about a belief. If our expectations on a particular trade are high, what does that actually mean? Simple. We are convinced that the underlying beliefs that the trade is based upon will work this time. What happens when a conviction or a strong belief is threatened? We experience anger and resentment against the source of the threat. If the source is another person, we typically respond with anger and attack the opponent who threatened our belief. We respond with anger because we learned that by doing so we were able to control the situation enough so that the person who questioned our belief decided to stop. Our opinion prevails because of the way we exercised control. Unfortunately the market cannot be controlled. This leaves us ultimately with uncontrollable fear.

CONTROLLING FEAR

So now that we have a working knowledge of fear, how can we control and eliminate it as best we can? The first step is to accept responsibility for our beliefs and actions, and what we value most. The second step is to accept that risk is a natural consequence of trading. Actually risk is a consequence of just waking up in the morning. In order to become outstanding in any human endeavor, we need to accept risk. When we are able to accept risk in everything we do, we can begin the process of changing our disempowering beliefs and references. The third step is to increase the beliefs that combat fear and decrease or eliminate the beliefs that encourage fear. The fourth and last step is to reexamine the beliefs and references that actually make us fearful. As we do, we can change our perception of them by asking intelligent questions.

As previously mentioned, questions have an incredible power to influence the ability of the mind to perceive new information. What beliefs and virtues would tend to decrease the amount of fear you could experience? Your beliefs about faith, confidence, discipline, courage, intuition, persistence, integrity, and flexibility would all tend to control the amount of fear you could experience. Is there a situation where you consistently experience fear while trading? If so, what thoughts are you experiencing? What beliefs are those thoughts based upon? Are your beliefs totally accurate? Are they empowering? What else could they mean? If you were to change a belief so that it was totally empowering, what would it be?

By using questions, we can begin to change the references that allow us to experience fear. As we change these references so they empower us, we will be less susceptible to fear. Finally, we must exercise discipline—to focus on beliefs that allow us to control fear and to remain focused on the desired outcome. Fear can disempower us only if we lack mental discipline to remain focused on what we desire and on the beliefs that enable us to accomplish our goals.

If you truly want to banish fear from controlling your life and your abilities as a trader, you must have the discipline to stay totally focused in the present moment. You experience fear when you have an undisciplined mind that allows you to focus either on references that caused you pain in the past or on potential new threats that may lead you to feel pain in the future.

Always remember that FEAR is nothing more than false evidence appearing real. Fear has a very hard time surviving when you discipline your mind to focus only on the present moment—and decide to take action.

12

ANGER: EASY TO FEEL, LIBERATING TO OVERCOME

The angry man will defeat himself in battle as well as in life.

—SAMURAI CODE

Whatever is begun in anger ends in shame.

—BENJAMIN FRANKLIN

THE MOST COMMON vice, or negative feeling, that novice traders experience on a consistent basis is anger. Even professional traders will at times experience anger. However, whereas novice traders will direct their anger at the market, their broker, or "the pit," professional traders will typically direct their anger more at themselves than at someone or something else.

Anger is an intense feeling of displeasure. Often the common behavior displayed is belligerence, where the angry individual becomes very hostile toward what is perceived to be the cause of pain. Many traders will attempt to punish or seek revenge against the market for their pain. The physiology of anger includes changes in breathing, body movement, and of course speech. In every part of the world, an angry person sticks out like a sore thumb—amazing in a way! Mentally an angry person is unable to think rational thoughts or perceive reality. This is why traders with an "attitude" will always blow up their account within a relatively short period of time.

There are a multitude of reasons that traders become angry. The most common is that their expectations were not fulfilled in the way they desired. As we have seen, a novice trader usually has many expectations on one trade. Typically the expectations are unrealistic, thus guaranteeing the trader more pain when the expectations are not met. This is in stark contrast to a professional trader, who normally has only one expectation on any one trade. Can you imagine what that expectation might be?

Another reason that traders are likely to become angry is that something they value (or need) is being violated or ignored. The most likely thing that is being violated is their equity or some highly valued belief. Highly valued beliefs among traders include the value of hard work, how success is obtained, how things should be, how perceptive or intelligent they are, and how great their methodology appears to be. In addition, if their basic needs are being violated or ignored, they will experience a lot of anger. If they are trading with money that they can't afford to lose (normally the case), they will become very angry when that money is lost.

In other words, if traders carefully develop and back-test a methodology over a period of months, and it proves to be very profitable on paper, they will come to value it highly. When they actually start trading it, they will be very proud of any profits they capture, and they will normally blame someone or something else for any losses. Now if their account starts to lose ever-increasing amounts of money, they will become fearful and then angry. This is because their methodology (something they value) is being threatened by the market (another perceptional belief). Since traders value their money, as it begins to decrease they will focus their anger on the market. In addition, if they also believe that hard work is required for success and their methodology (which took a lot of hard work) is creating losses, it represents not only a threat against their approach and their equity, but also a threat against the belief that hard work brings success.

This leads us to the third most common reason that traders get angry—their beliefs are being violated or not being met. When a methodology that works on paper fails in practice, traders experience ever-increasing levels of anger and fear. This is because not only are their expectations of profit and their highly valued methodology being violated, but the underlying beliefs that their methodology is based upon are also being trashed. How could such an approach be so successful when back-tested and yet such a loser in real time? As their level of confusion and fear increases, the intensity of their anger will also increase as they unconsciously try to control the situation and reduce the fear. Unfortunately, the market doesn't care and is immune to human anger and any efforts to control it.

In short, traders experience ever-increasing levels of anger because their level of understanding is insufficient to comprehend the demands of the market. They do not understand how to control their beliefs or how to increase their virtues. As the intensity of their anger increases, it further diminishes their ability to accurately perceive the market.

Whenever you get angry, you are remembering past references where by getting angry you were able to control (or at least influence) the outcome. In all probability you attached a certain amount of significance to being angry that helped you favorably affect the outcome. The only problem is that when you are trading and you get angry, instead of gaining some control, you lose all control. The market doesn't care if you are seething with anger or totally joyous.

When you are angry, you lose any semblance of objectivity regarding the market. Consequently, as the intensity of anger increases, the level of objectivity decreases. What causes this decrease in objectivity? What controls your perceptions? That's right, beliefs. Can you remember a time when you were very angry about either the market or something else altogether? What were you focusing on? What beliefs were you linking to being angry? Why did it feel like you were justified?

In order for you to experience anger with less frequency and intensity, you must change the beliefs that you have about anger and the beliefs that you link to anger. As you know by now, the way to do so is to ask questions to create doubt about the validity of your original belief, then decide to (1) keep the belief as it is, (2) modify it, or (3) discard it and adopt a new belief that empowers you. Many traders have linked a belief regarding anger that they think empowers them. For example, they may say, "I know that anger is bad, but at times I am justified, and it gives me the strength to get my viewpoint across." To change such a belief, they will have to ask questions that create doubt about its validity. Then they must link a new belief to anger that actually empowers them. Some questions they could ask are: "What about this situation makes me think that I am justified about getting angry? What about this situation might be misrepresented? How could I be perceiving this situation incorrectly? What beliefs am I using to come to this decision? Am I representing the references accurately? Am I perceiving this situation accurately?" A new empowering belief could be that anytime they experience anger they are losing the ability to perceive the situation rationally, and by doing so they are the ultimate loser.

The primary way to control anger is by adopting better beliefs about anger, about accepting the risk that is inherent in the marketplace, and about the true nature of the markets. As noted earlier, the physiology of anger is unique, and transcends all cultures. Your physiology affects the quality of the beliefs that you are currently experiencing, and your current beliefs affect your physiology—it becomes a vicious circle. As you begin to increase your virtues and the quality of your beliefs, you will have the ability to get out of the state of anger and to avoid it by *deciding* either to change the beliefs you are focusing upon or to change your physiology. How angry do you think you could remain if you took a deep breath, smiled (not grimaced), and slowly stretched your muscles? Might you be stretching your mental abilities as well? Would the intensity level remain the same or decrease?

Just as with fear, anger is very difficult to experience when we are focused in the present moment. This is because in order to experience anger we have to think about how our beliefs, values, or expectations are not being met. The act of thinking about how our beliefs were "violated" requires us to remove ourselves from the present moment and reflect on our beliefs. When we are trading, we must exist in the present moment; consequently any feelings of anger that might be experienced will be felt only when we are done trading.

What this means is that to experience anger with less frequency and intensity, we must control our beliefs about the justification and value of anger. As we strengthen our virtues and our empowering beliefs, the anger we experience will begin to diminish. The best virtue that we can use to combat anger is forgiveness. When we have the ability to truly forgive, we are capable of instantly exiting an angry state. This is especially true when we are angry at ourselves.

By focusing on your mental abilities to control your beliefs, you can determine how perceptive you will become. When you realize the damage that uncontrolled fear and anger can do to your emotional, physical, and financial well-being, you will constantly strive to eliminate them.

13

DOUBT AND INDECISION—A SUREFIRE WAY TO RUIN

Losing a position is aggravating, whereas losing your nerve is devastating.

—ED SEYKOTA

The greatest risk is to do nothing.

—JERRY RAFFERTY

Our doubts are traitors and make us lose the good we might win, by fearing to attempt.

—WILLIAM SHAKESPEARE

THE CONSEQUENCE OF experiencing fear and anger on a fairly consistent basis is doubt. When we experience doubt, we also experience indecision. A trader who is experiencing indecision will hesitate to "pull the trigger" and enter the market.

Doubt is a thought that questions the possibility of an outcome being realized or the validity of a belief. A trader whose particular belief about the market is repeatedly violated will begin to doubt that the belief is valid. In addition, the trader will begin to question if sought-after profits will ever be realized.

Traders who are experiencing doubt feel uncertainty, distrust, and disbelief. The uncertainty arises because they are no longer certain of the outcome. Uncertain of the validity of their thoughts or beliefs, they will come to doubt their actions. The feeling of distrust usually arises because their faith in beliefs and skills that can lead to an expected outcome is in question. In addition, they may distrust the intentions or abilities of others. In other words, traders experience distrust because they begin to question the validity of their beliefs, abilities, or goals. The feeling of disbelief arises because traders are experiencing astonishment that the event or the action of the market even occurred. The disbelief stems in large part from their inability to accept that the market is behaving the way it is.

Doubt originates in both our conscious and unconscious mind. When it originates in our unconscious mind, it is usually based on our intuitive sense. That is, the unconscious mind senses that something is not quite right with the picture being presented to our conscious mind. When doubt originates in our conscious mind, it is usually because the part of our mind that controls critical thinking abilities is questioning either our beliefs about the event or the event itself. That is, we are using preexisting knowledge to critically think about the overall validity of our beliefs.

Often we experience doubt when we lack certainty or lose trust in ourselves or others. Very often the more fear we experience, the more doubt we experience as well. Traders who experience a series of severe losses after laboriously devising a trading methodology are typically astonished that the losses could even take place. They are amazed at the action of their methodology and the market. This feeling of astonishment is a sense of disbelief, which will in turn create even more uncertainty about producing consistent profits. Often this disbelief will cause traders to distrust their abilities to perceive the market correctly and the validity of their beliefs.

When the doubt becomes overwhelming, traders will often stop pursuing the goal of increasing their equity by trading.

The end result of doubt, for novice traders, is that they become very skeptical about their abilities and are alienated from the market. Alienation further increases the likelihood that they will never create a valid trading strategy. Professional traders use their skepticism to motivate themselves to learn about doubt, to ask new questions, and to change their perceptions, thereby creating better beliefs. Doubt always leads to more uncertainty, which in turn creates more doubt. When traders realize that they must change their beliefs on trading because they are experiencing doubt, then the doubt actually motivates them to create new beliefs and therefore to regain their sense of certainty.

The biggest consequence of doubt is indecision. Like a departing ship, the market waits for no one. Traders who have doubts are unable to make a trade when they need to—before the ship leaves the pier. Whenever traders say they knew the market was about to go up and missed the move, it is because of doubt—typically they lost trust in their abilities or beliefs about the market, or experienced different levels of fear. Whenever you find it difficult to enter a trade, you must take the time to ascertain the reason you are experiencing doubt. Then you must change the limiting belief or create enough references that will allow you to trust the validity of your thoughts.

Doubt will cause you to be indecisive, hesitating before entering or exiting the market. Indecision is the inability to act or to decide. Indecision is caused by fear, doubt, and a lack of strong virtues and empowering beliefs. Traders in an indecisive state normally feel discomfort and deep apprehension.

Indecisive traders will always produce inconsistent behavior, and consequently inconsistent profits. Yet indecision is the precise point where traders' opportunity to grow is at its best. If they decide to use the experience to overcome their limiting beliefs and behaviors, they will be on the road to success. However, if they fail to take decisive action, there is a good chance that they will learn how to be helpless. Or they may become forever trapped in an "approach-avoidance conflict."

The first trap—learned helplessness—is an interesting psychological concept. It is best captured by analogy. In India when elephant trainers desire to train elephants to obey human commands, they begin with a baby elephant. They tie a stout rope to one leg of the baby elephant, and then secure the rope to a strong stake in the ground. The elephant will struggle to free itself and finally give up in exhaustion. Within a relatively short period of time the animal ceases struggling. The trainer continues to use a rope at night so the elephant doesn't wander off. The amazing thing is that a fully grown elephant could easily pull the stake out of the ground, or break the rope, yet doesn't even attempt to free itself. The elephant has learned to be helpless, because it continues to think (consciously and/or unconsciously) that its actions are doomed—so why try?

Similarly, when traders experience doubt and indecision, and if they fail to exert themselves to take decisive action, they are slowly learning how to be helpless! Traders who have learned to be helpless are convinced that their beliefs have no effect on outcomes. They honestly believe that despite all effort, they will never improve, that they are not in charge of their own trading destiny. Thus begins the vicious circle: Traders must change in order to break out of their learned helplessness, yet what they have learned is not to change.

The other trap—the approach-avoidance conflict—is also best explained by analogy. Hungry rats have an intense desire for food, especially as they grow more hungry, but simultaneously will develop a repulsion for the food if while approaching the food they receive electric shocks in varying amounts. They associate food with the pain of being shocked. The distance that the rats stay away from the food is determined by how hungry they are and the amount of electricity used to shock them. The rats want to approach the food, and simultaneously want to avoid it. The rats will finally approach and eat the food when the pain of the possible random electric shocks is less than the hunger pains.

Thus traders fear the random pain that the market can create by making them wrong and by threatening their beliefs and values. However, they desire the pleasure of making money. An interesting thing about profits is that within a short-term time frame a trader's profits will appear to be random. The trader will never know if the next trade will be a winner or a loser. Random profits (or rewards) are highly addictive to the psyche. (Why do you think slot machines are so popular?) In addition to desiring profits, traders like to obtain validation for their beliefs about the market.

Traders who develop an approach-avoidance conflict become very indecisive. Like the hungry rat, they will mentally stand a safe distance away from the object of their desire, but as desire increases they will move closer to it. Their focus is on what they desire and fear, and true to form they will eventually enter the trade, forgetting their discipline and possibly getting rewarded, but definitely experiencing mental pain.

In order to avoid falling into either the learned helplessness or approach-avoidance trap, traders must change their perceptions of the market. The pain they experience is within their own mind; their perceptions about the market, not the market itself, are generating the pain. To overcome this situation, traders need to strengthen their virtues and empowering beliefs on a daily, consistent basis.

Your goal is to become as objective about the market as possible. Some of the enabling beliefs you should possess are to feel no pressure or fear to enter any particular trade and no sense of rejection or anger on making a losing trade, you know that there is no right or wrong—only outcomes. You have the discipline always to undertake a particular action if the market is presenting a particular pattern. You are focused on the structure of the market in the time frame you are trading in, not on making money. You have already decided in advance what action to undertake in particular situations. You have released yourself from the need to be right, and don't care what the market does.

14

LOSING MONEY: THE TRADER'S COST OF DOING BUSINESS

Don't expect to be right all the time. If you have made a mistake, cut your losses as quickly as possible.

—BERNARD BARUCH

Being wrong is good information, too—it tells you that you are either early, or that you should reverse opinion.

—TOM R. PETERSON

I N ORDER TO become a successful trader, you must change your perception of what a loss means. There will be trades that generate a loss of equity—this is a cold, hard truth. The meaning that traders attach to that loss, however, will be determined by their perception, which in turn is influenced by their beliefs and the emotional intensity they attach to the loss. Since the vast majority of traders have an inherent resistance to acknowledging a losing trade, you must adopt the belief that you want to acknowledge a losing trade as quickly as possible. Otherwise the resultant stress and anxiety will prevent you from accomplishing your goal.

The amount of money you consistently produce will depend on forcing yourself to represent a loss in an empowering way.

The stress and anxiety that most traders feel is caused by the failure to strengthen their nine virtues. It is also caused by thinking either consciously or unconsciously that the market conforms to some logical, predicative, and reasonable rules (as yet to be discovered by the trader). It bears repeating that excellent traders have come to the realization that the market is a never-ending event. Excellent traders believe that the market behaves with absolutely no regard for their financial position.

In many ways the market is like stormy ocean waves. Each wave is unique, the exact characteristic of the wave cannot be predicted, the variations are endless, the waves are endless, and there is no beginning, middle, or end to the amount of water crashing on the beach. Similarly each trade you enter is unique, the exact characteristics of the trade cannot be predicted, the variations of the price action are endless, the price action never ceases, and the market is constantly washing away the novice traders.

Everybody tells the new trader to let profits run, and cut losses short. It seems that everyone has a "system" or a "course" to sell you. There are countless ways to generate a stop loss price, an exit price, and an entry price. It seems that all you have to do to make lots of money is to find the right system. The truth is that the real work of trading is performed in the space between your ears. The amount of pain you experience when you lose money is a good indication of how much work you must perform to change your beliefs about the market and your perception of a loss.

The amount of pain that you place on a losing trade is the result of your focus and beliefs. One trader might become very upset at losing $500, while another trader would not even be slightly perturbed. The reason is that the internal representation of what $500 means is vastly different to the two traders. Likewise, if you believe that a loss is caused by the failure of the market to behave in the correct manner, you will get extremely upset when it behaves unexpectedly. However, another trader who believes an occasional loss is unavoidable, and is the cost of finding out the validity of his or her perception, will not get upset.

When I first started trading commodities, my younger brother Frank (who had been trading natural gas for years at various companies in Houston) posed the following situation to me: There are two day traders in natural gas. During the day one trader goes short and the other goes long. At the end of the day the long trader has made money, and the short trader has lost money. Who has the right methodology? My answer was, naturally, the profitable trader. His answer was that, based upon one trade, it was impossible to say which trader was correct; only the market was right. The response bothered and confused me for quite a while. Frank explained it this way: The long trader went long for his reasons, and the short trader had her reasons. Both traders in all probability had the wrong reasons. The market was the only player who absolutely knew the correct reason, and the market always does the right thing. The long trader, although profitable, was able to hitch a ride in the profitable direction *possibly* because of his ability to see the market action correctly, but this didn't validate his methodology based upon the one trade.

I argued that the long trader was profitable because he was able to see the market correctly, and profit accordingly. Frank's response was that it was more luck than skill in that one particular trade. The key word here is "particular." An outstanding trader with the "right" methodology will consistently make money over a sample of many trades. Please let me repeat this with emphasis: *An outstanding trader is consistently profitable over many trades.* Remember that novice trades will determine their success in a very myopic way.

If outstanding traders are profitable over a length of time, how do you think they will represent a losing trade? What emotions will they experience when they have a loss? What will they feel, and what will their inner voice be saying? Now for the kicker, what will they feel after several consecutive losing trades? I will answer these questions shortly; however, I suspect that many of you already know the answer!

Here is another situation. Let's say you are watching wheat being traded, and if we could stop time for a minute, what does the last traded price (say, 209.25) represent to you? A successful trader will answer that it represents the consensus of opinion about the value of wheat in this instant of time, remembering the past and anticipating the future on the basis of all the traders trading at the moment. Now let us allow time to advance a split second, and in that length of time two new traders (A and B) make a trade at 210.25, one going short and the other going long. How does this affect the perception of traders A and B? Well, they both believe that their perception is correct. If they did not both believe they were right, then they would not have taken opposing positions. Did the previous continuity of thought have anything to do with the present continuity of bullish thought? Possibly, depending on why the two traders executed their trades. However, it is possible that the two traders made their trades on the basis of information that previous traders had no knowledge of. In fact, traders A and B might not even care what happened in the past because they both believe that something is going to happen in the future. It is impossible for us to determine. Did these two new traders affect the continuity of thought of the previous traders? Of course. The long traders are happy, and the short traders are upset that they are losing! The longs are thinking that they are smart, and very much on top of the hill. Now if we allow time to advance another split second, and two more traders (C and D) execute a trade at 211.25, what happens to the perception of the first two traders (A and B)? It has changed. Now both traders no longer think they are correct. The trader with the bullish perspective is happy and convinced that she is right, while the trader with the bearish perspective is upset that the price continues to go higher, and has some anxiety that he might have made a mistake.

What can we learn from this? Simple. What the previous longs and shorts believed, expected, rationalized, and predicted was ultimately determined by two traders agreeing on a price *possibly* based on previously known information. However, they could have agreed on a new price because of new information, opinions, or expectations of future events. The point is that the market is always right, and that it is totally unpredictable. It will occasionally appear to respect previous support, and resistance points, that you see on your chart. In doing so, it is validating your beliefs about support and resistance levels. At other times it will blow right through those prices as though they are totally meaningless. What you, your computer program, or your newsletter believes, thinks, or expects is of no consequence in the overall direction of the market. No matter how large your bankroll is, the market will always be larger. Even countries that have tried to artificially maintain high (or low) valuations of their currencies (Japan, Malaysia, Indonesia, Britain, Russia, Brazil) have discovered that the market is too large to manipulate for any length of time.

An interesting question arises. If the markets can't be manipulated long term by the central banks of various countries with all their immense resources (financial, intellectual, and physical), can the markets ever be manipulated? The answer is that the markets can be manipulated only when there is no continuity of thought. Whenever the market is undecided, a large enough trader (individual, corporate, or government) can enter the market and bully the price up or down. It must be stressed that the reason this is possible is that the market is uncertain about future events. There is no continuity of thought. Whenever the market is exhibiting a certain continuity of (bullish or bearish) thought about where it is heading, no one can bully the market around.

Successful traders see price movements as an opportunity to buy low and sell high (or vice versa), or buy high and sell higher (or vice versa). Their goal is to perceive a pattern of some sort that will allow them to determine a value relative to a future point in time. A successful trader knows that the market is an entity that is never wrong, and exists to provide participants with a way to profit. An outstanding trader is striving to consistently make profits over a series of trades. Although a particular trade in a particular market will be unpredictable, when considered in the aggregate, certain probabilities in favor of a trader with an "edge" may be established that will allow consistent profitability.

Now to answer the previous question. Successful traders will in most cases experience no negative emotions when they place a trade that results in a loss. Even after consecutive losing trades, they will continue to experience no negative emotions! Why? Because successful traders believe that the market is always correct at this exact instant of time; and if the last trade resulted in a loss, then one of two things are transpiring in the marketplace. First, the market is changing direction. While the trader's perception is indicating that the market is heading in one direction, the market is actually going in the opposite direction, resulting in the loss. In other words, if the trader perceives that the market is heading down and experiences a loss from being short, the market is indicating that the perception is wrong. Second, the market is not certain where it is heading, there is no continuity of thought, and there is a battle under way between the bears and the bulls—with the resultant increase in volatility and resultant loss.

The reason successful traders do not get angry, fearful, and resentful about their loss is that they have mastered the virtues and beliefs that trading demands. They represent the market in a way that allows them to define the market action, and their own action, in a very clear and precise manner.

They can very clearly define their behavior because of their internal values, beliefs, and rules.

Now am I saying that successful traders never get upset? Hardly. They do get upset. However, they have the ability to represent being upset in a way that strengthens their abilities, beliefs, and virtues. Upon experiencing a loss (or a series of losses) that causes their perceptions to become destabilized, successful traders will often close out their positions. They will then do something that allows them to put some time between that loss and the next trading decision. By allowing some time to elapse, they can question the internal representation that their mind is currently experiencing. By asking intelligent questions about why their perceptions became destabilized, they are able to make better, more empowering distinctions.

Novice traders are tempted to avoid thinking about the market when they become upset. Professional traders know that whenever they want to avoid thinking about the market, it is the exact time to begin questioning their perceptions of the market. Excellent traders know that they cannot let losing trades bother them emotionally. When they recognize that they are on a losing streak, they trim down their activity and wait it out. Professional traders believe that attempting to trade with the same number of contracts or with the same frequency during a losing streak is emotionally exhausting. Their goal is to start seeing black ink on a consistent basis, before scaling back up to their regular number of contracts or frequency of trading. Outstanding traders are able to acknowledge that the losing trade occurred in the past, allowing them to make new distinctions so they may refine their methodology. By placing no emotional energy into a losing trade, they are able to more accurately perceive the losing trade. Successful traders are always focused on the instant of time they are trading in, and what they are going to do to profit from the price action. While they are actually trading, they forget what happened in the past until the trading day is over—to do otherwise is to change focus from the present to the past. They know that focusing on the past while trading only guarantees future losses.

So how do novice traders change their beliefs about a loss? How do they get rid of the anger, pain, and resentment they feel toward the market? Once again, the way it is done is by realizing that every time these negative emotions come up they must be placed into a constructive context. Half the battle is realizing that the negative beliefs must change. The other half of the battle is to take the time and energy to change them. By using the techniques already mentioned, you will be able to change old beliefs and create new beliefs that prevent you from using your old beliefs. Do you know what your beliefs about the market are?

Ask any great traders what trade made them the happiest and why, and they will tell you several things came together. First, their methodology indicated a particular trade, and they acted upon it without any fear, hesitation, or anxiety. Second, they controlled their emotions and monitored the price movement while in the trade, and exited the trade exactly when their methodology indicated. Third, they were in the "zone." Finally, they made a killing on the trade.

Should a trade not be profitable, professional traders will say that it was unfortunate that it did not work out. The reason they aren't upset even though the trade lost money is that they entered into the trade, monitored everything while in the trade, and at the right time according to their own rules exited the trade. *All* with no emotional involvement. The fact that they lost some money is of little concern. *Losing money on a trade is the cost of doing business—it is to be expected.*

How does this compare with the response of a novice trader? Ask novices about a great trade, and they will tell you about the killing they made in soybeans the other day. Ask why they made a killing, and they will not be able to tell you exactly what had to happen to make them enter into the trade. Do you see how the focus of an experienced trader and a novice trader is totally different.

Novice traders focus on how much money they might make and how much they might lose. Experienced traders focus on all the steps required to fanatically obey their methodology. This difference in attitude is very real; yet many people explain it away by saying that successful traders are being modest or aloof, or deliberately vague so that they won't divulge their trading secrets. Professional traders are all too willing to confront the truth about their virtues and vices, so that they can confront the market with a tranquil mind.

What usually upsets great traders is the failure to obey their own rules. Just as novice traders get upset when they lose money, more experienced traders get upset when they fail to follow their own methodology and rules. Anger and resentment can be controlled by strengthening the trading virtues and creating empowering beliefs.

The amount of money you are able to create is merely a by-product of your trading skills. Likewise, the amount of money you manage to lose indicates how much your trading skills need to be improved. Trading skills involve mastery of your virtues, vices, and beliefs, and mastery of a unique way of perceiving the market. The bottom line is that in actuality the amount of money that you create is indicative of how much your perceptions are accurate and insightful and your beliefs are empowering. One of my beliefs is that it is a waste of time to attempt to explain *why* the market did this or that. I am far more interested in *what* the market is doing *right now.* I am really interested in determining what the probable direction of the market might be. The reason I never predict the market, and instead work in probabilities, is that if I predict, I am putting a certain amount of emotional energy into the prediction and my ego starts to get involved. When I work in probabilities, my ego is barely involved, I have acknowledged that the markets are unpredictable, and I am emotionally detaching myself from the action of the market.

Highly successful traders believe that the market is totally unpredictable, and that the market represents all the beliefs, perceptions, and fears of participants in a given instant of time. Consequently, occasional losses are to be expected. Successful traders also believe that the market doesn't owe them any validation of their perceptions—it just flat out doesn't care. They believe that the market is always right, and that consistent losses indicate their perception is wrong. This requires them to question their beliefs and where they are focusing. They must then change the disempowering beliefs so they become empowering. Since the market is always right, and *they have no expectations of the market (only of themselves),* loss has no emotional feelings linked to it.

Successful traders believe that the amount of loss can be reduced by using strict rules that have been validated through testing. They are willing to be flexible in looking at new ideas that could affect their perceptions. A loss has no negative emotions linked to it because some loss is unavoidable and is the natural consequence of trading. In short, successful traders have no negative emotions linked to loss because they have totally accepted responsibility for their own actions. They have accepted in their very being that trading demands working in probabilities. Thus occasional losses are to be expected.

Contrast this approach with the most common beliefs of novice traders: that the market can be analyzed and predicted, that it is reasonable, and that market action repeats. Consequently these traders have a lot of expectations. When they experience a loss, they experience pain. Novice traders invariably believe that the way to avoid feeling any pain is to become more knowledgeable about the different methods of analyzing the market. Consequently they invest even more time and emotional energy into discovering the "underlying truth" about the market. They create even more expectations. Naturally enough, this creates more pain as the losses continue. Novice traders do extensive work to obtain more information so that they can devise a better methodology; however, they do not consistently apply the methodology. So when a loss comes along, they are unable to point an accusing finger at their methodology because they failed to use it consistently. So they do the only logical thing—point their finger at the market. The result is that they expect the market to validate their research by giving them profits. It is any wonder that novice traders get so fearful, angry, doubtful, hesitant, and frustrated with the market? Is it any wonder that they burn out so quickly?

Successful traders obtain consistent profits. Losing traders obtain consistent pain. In order to become the trader you desire, you must change the internal representations of what a loss means. You must diligently apply yourself to mastering your perceptions, believing with certainty that you will transform yourself into an outstanding trader, have the discipline to develop and obey your trading methodology, have the courage to execute your methodology without hesitation, have the wisdom to differentiate between "into wishing" and intuition, have the persistence never to quit, have the integrity to stand apart from other traders, and have the mental flexibility to be open-minded. If you do, I promise you that at some point in time you will represent a loss in such a way that you will become a highly profitable trader.

15

CONSISTENT PROFITS COME FROM EMPOWERING BELIEFS

Money is the most important thing in the world. It represents health, strength, honor, generosity, and beauty as conspicuously as the want of it represents illness, weakness, disgrace, meanness, and ugliness.

—GEORGE BERNARD SHAW

The use of money is all the advantage there is in having money.

—BENJAMIN FRANKLIN

ONSISTENT PROFITS COME when a trader is able to consistently see the market as it is. *Consistent profits result from taking consistent action.* The underlying requirement is the ability to perceive the market correctly. As we know, perception is an interpretive act that is influenced by traders' beliefs, values, and expectations. When traders are able to perceive the market correctly, they will be able to create a trading methodology that gives them an "edge," or slight advantage over other traders.

It all starts with traders increasing their virtues. They must become more virtuous. I know that in this time and age virtue sounds a bit old-fashioned. But by becoming more virtuous, traders will be able to increase their empowering references and create better and more empowering beliefs.

Let's review again some of the key beliefs that successful traders have about the market. They believe that the market is always correct—that the price is where it should be. The market represents the psychology of all traders in any instant of time. The most valid moves are when the market shifts and there is no obvious explanation why. The market will always behave in an unexpected manner. The market is not like life—it is much more discontinuous than continuous. Never argue with the market—unless you want to lose. The market will always go where it wants to. These are just a few beliefs of successful traders.

In short, the market can do anything, at any time, for any reason, the market is always right, and the market doesn't even know the individual traders exist. The most common beliefs that successful traders have about themselves is that they are responsible for their own actions, beliefs, perceptions, and risks, and they must devise their own trading methodology. In their view, trading methodology gives them part of their edge, and perception gives them the rest of their edge.

Just as traders have general beliefs about the market, they also have specific beliefs about what it takes to generate consistent profits. They also represent a winning trade differently from novice traders. Successful traders have specific beliefs that allow them to represent a loss so that it is empowering. Successful traders also represent a profit so that it empowers their belief structure. I can hear many of you saying, "Wait a second, John. All my wins empower me!" If this is so, then why is it so difficult for a novice trader to exit from a winning trade?

The reason is fear. Novice traders have a deep fear of exiting a winning trade because it could go higher. If it did go higher, they would be "leaving money on the table." When novice traders initially enter a trade, they are focusing on how much money they could lose and on how much money the market could give them. When the trade becomes profitable, their focus changes. They are now concerned about how much money the market can take away. Everything they do arises from a state of fear. *Any decision a trader makes while experiencing fear is almost guaranteed to give an undesirable outcome.*

We have already examined the majority of disempowering beliefs held by novice traders. Are there any others? Not really. The only disempowering belief that I should mention again in this chapter is the notion that the market is responsible for a trader's profits or losses. Novice traders honestly believe that better market analysis will give them more consistent profits—that they can predict the behavior of the market. In other words, they believe that by increasing their ability to consistently predict market behavior, they will be able to obtain consistent profits. Most novice traders have a very narrow focus. They allow the market action to determine their attitude.

The vast majority of novice traders lack the discipline to always obey their methodology and money management rules. Lack of discipline means they can avoid taking responsibility for their actions. They believe that they have accepted the risk of trading by using a stop loss order, which is definitely not the case. In short, novice traders are trading mentally from a state of fear, which is occasionally negated by euphoria.

Novice traders experience euphoria whenever they have a large winning trade. I know what it feels like. After I had traded commodities for a few years, my methodology indicated that I should establish a short position in bonds. I went short, and several days later bonds went limit down. My brother Frank called the morning they went limit down, and I can still remember how euphoric I felt as I talked with him. I exited the position the next day with considerable profits. The question to ask is: Was it the market that made me right, or was it my beliefs and consequently my perception that the market was rolling over that allowed me to take the action my methodology was indicating? Some of you may be thinking in the back of your head, "What's so wrong with euphoria?"

So what is so wrong about euphoria? Easy. The next time I made a trade, was it a winner or loser? If you answered that I lost money you are correct. In fact, it took five consecutive trades before I had a profit. Five consecutive unprofitable trades is a lot for me; consequently I was not a very happy trader. My ability to perceive the market correctly was initially being affected by my euphoria, and then by my sense of dejection at losing on subsequent trades. An amazing thing about the market is that it will bring you back to reality very fast—often whether you want to or not.

Euphoria is very pleasant, uplifting, and inspirational. But it is an emotion that a trader must avoid while trading. This is because euphoria will prevent you from perceiving the market as it is. Often euphoria will give you an emotional feeling of invulnerability. If you begin to believe that every trade you make is a winner, you are allowing your unconscious mind to overwhelm your conscious ability to reason. In short, your ego is now making the trading decisions, and as you know this is very bad for your equity. Euphoria is crippling to a trader's abilities because it is such a strong emotion. Anger and euphoria affect your ability to perceive the market to the same degree.

The best thing a trader can do while under the influence of either anger or euphoria is to mentally shift gears until these emotions no longer influence the conscious or unconscious mind.

An important point I need to stress here concerns learning. A few paragraphs back I mentioned how novice traders believe that becoming better at market analysis will lead to consistent profits. The implication is that more market knowledge means more consistent profits. *Consistent profits originate from valid beliefs—not knowledge of the market.* I would like to expand on this point. Novice traders fail to obtain consistent profits with more knowledge of the markets because of their underlying beliefs. The chief underlying belief is that by obtaining more knowledge they will be able to control their risk, and more reliably predict where the price is going. Novice traders are attempting to control their fear (risk) by more knowledge. They are attempting to meet certain primary needs. They want to satisfy their needs for certainty (the ability to determine where the price is going), for variety (increasing the variables they examine), and for significance (more complicated or esoteric indicators).

Novice traders are on a quest for more knowledge in an attempt to eliminate the pain the market can inflict. They want to eliminate the amount or intensity of the fear they are experiencing. The problem is that they are doomed to failure. The more esoteric their indicators become—and the more powerful their computers—the more they are attempting to escape from accepting responsibility.

Let me ask you a few questions. Do you think the market will exist 100 years from now? Do you think that our technological abilities will be much more advanced? Do you think that novice traders in the future will be using much more advanced computers, computer models, and indicators than they are today? Why are they using these new "tools"?

Am I saying that more computing power is counterproductive, that becoming more knowledgeable about the market or using esoteric mathematical formulas is a bad thing? Hardly! It is a bad thing if the underlying reason is an attempt to escape from accepting responsibility. It is not a bad thing if the underlying reason is to increase the trader's edge. Traders increase their edge when they can see the underlying truth or structure of the market. I know this sounds like I am splitting hairs—however, let me assure you that I am not.

Consider this analogy. A man who helps an elderly woman across the street at night because he remembers his grandmother, and is acting from his virtues, is entirely different from a man who intends to mug the woman when she gets into the darkness on the other side of the street. The action is the same, but the intent is totally different, as is the outcome. Traders who have accepted responsibility for their own outcome, accepted the risk, and adopted some arcane notion of market action in order to obtain a larger edge are not strengthening their disempowering beliefs about the market. This is in stark contrast to traders who are learning because they want to eliminate fear by being able to accurately predict prices. These traders are strengthening their disempowering beliefs without realizing it. As in a lot of things, the intent or underlying belief that caused the action is everything.

Consistently profitable traders possess certain common beliefs about profits. Successful traders believe that profits come to them because they are able to perceive the market as it is. The better their perception, the greater their profit. They think in probabilities, and they know that in time their edge "methodology" will allow them to realize consistent profits. Since they work in probabilities, and since the market will do the unexpected, they will have losses as well as profits. Just as they have no emotional attachment to a loss, they have little emotional attachment to a profit.

Successful traders perceive the market not as a threat, but as a vehicle (do you remember what a vehicle is?) that allows them to make money. In the vast majority of cases they realize that fear is caused by their beliefs. So if they are experiencing fear, they begin to ask questions about what beliefs are causing the fear, and then change the beliefs. This allows them to perceive the market action without being under the influence of fear. In fact, they experience no fear, anger, doubt, or indecision while trading. They are not experiencing any stress because they have accepted responsibility for the consequences of their beliefs, perceptions, and actions, and because they are existing only in the moment—they are in the "zone."

Outstanding traders are able to generate consistent profits because they have the ability and skill to behave consistently. They consistently fill their mind with empowering beliefs, they are consistently able to perceive the true action of the market, they consistently obey their trading methodology and risk control rules, they consistently predefine where they are entering or exiting and the dollar amount risked, they are consistently flexible in their approach, and they consistently ask themselves intelligent, empowering questions.

There is no other way to create consistent profits!

The Strategies of Successful Trading

THE STRATEGY
OF DETERMINING
THE MARKET
CONSENSUS

*The prices of stocks, commodities, and bonds are affected by
literally anything and everything that happens in our
world....What registers are not the events themselves but the
human reactions to these events, how millions of individuals
feel these happenings may affect the future!*

—BERNARD BARUCH

I CAN HEAR some of you saying, "At last. John is finally going to get off this psychological stuff and get into something that I can sink my teeth into, that I can program." Well you are partially correct. I would like to share with you a strategy that is the cornerstone of the technical analysis that I do while trading. Although I use more esoteric mathematical models to trade with, they are founded upon the concepts in this chapter. Your goal is to devise your own methodology—not to use someone else's. The purpose of your methodology is to help you perceive the market as it is, thereby giving you your "edge." It is not to devise some esoteric model as an end, but rather as a means to enhance your perception.

Some of you may brush this chapter off as too rudimentary, and not sophisticated enough. However, every methodology must have a solid foundation to build upon. This is my foundation. Although this chapter is important, it is of far less importance than the first chapter on mastering your ego and beliefs. I have taken the liberty of assuming that you already have a fair understanding of technical analysis, and the terminology used in technical analysis.

Bernard Baruch was born on August 19, 1870, and went on to become a trader. He made a large fortune from trading stocks and commodities—starting in the late 1800s and ending in the 1940s. I first heard the expression "continuity of thought" while reading Baruch's autobiography. Baruch first heard it from Middleton Burrill, another stock trader who remarked about a break in a rising market in the late 1890s. "That collapse is going to break the continuity of bullish thought," said Burrill.

It is the best way I have found to describe the psychology that is moving a market. It is amazing to me that novice traders think that the traders making millions somehow have an inside line on what is taking place. The information available to the professional trader is in most cases the same information available to the novice. Although professionals may subscribe to some expensive advisory services, the bulk of their information comes from the market action, newspapers, magazines, and the Internet. The reason professional traders are able to interpret the information so they can profit, and the novice remains totally ignorant, is that professional traders have mastered their beliefs and virtues. In addition, professionals have mastered *their ability to think.* All too often the novice trader confuses information with thinking.

Throughout this part of the book I will mention support and resistance points. The vast majority of traders have an instinctive reflex that associates "trend" with a bull market. When they think of "support" they think of it within the context of a bull market, and "resistance" within the context of a bull market. Since this book is a reflection of how I think, you will need to understand that when I mention "support" it could be in the context of either a *bull or bear market.* The same is true for "resistance." When I think of a trend, I see it in my mind's eye as consisting of two forces—the buyers and the sellers, or the bears and the bulls, or the forces of supply and demand, or the white stones and black stones from a GO board. Neither force is morally superior to the other; *they just exist.* Regardless of how you represent them, there will always be two forces, one that is dominant and one that is submissive yet rebellious. The dominant force will have certain price levels that serve as support to continued advancement, and yet other price levels that act as resistance to advancement.

In other words, resistance for the bulls is a price level that the bulls have a difficult time getting above. Resistance for the bears is a price level that the bears have a difficult time getting under. Support is a price level that the bulls retreat back to, and find the support of more bulls willing to buy at the lower price. Support for the bears is a price level that the bears can retreat back to, and find the support of more bears willing to sell at the higher price. A resistance price level for the stronger side is a support area for the weaker side. I fully understand that this view is totally different from the view of most traders. I arrived at my perspective after playing a lot of GO.

Occasionally I will say that if a price is violated, then the stronger force just lost. This is best described by an example. Suppose the current price is 100 and the bulls have established 98 as a support level. If the bears close under 98, then I would say that 98 was violated and the bears are in charge. Most of my methodology is based on the close of whatever time frame I am trading in; consequently an intraday price of 97 and a close of 99 would not count as a violation if I am trading off daily charts. While this may seem elementary to some readers, the concept is critical.

The truth is that all traders see the same prices; however, their perception of what those prices mean is different. All traders see the price move up and then down, but the *meaning* they attach to that movement is different. The truth of the matter is that the meaning you attach to the price movement is determined by your perception. Your perception is influenced by your beliefs, values, and physiology. Your beliefs and values are determined by your experiences or references on what this price movement means to you.

For example, can you remember the first time you ever saw a price chart? When you saw that first chart, were you aware of what a retracement was or what a double bottom was? Did you know what support or resistance was, and what it signified? In all probability you didn't have a clue. When I first started trading Eastman Kodak, DuPont, and IBM stock back in

1975, I had no idea what a candlestick was. Today I look only at charts using candlesticks! At the time that I was using trend lines, retracements, and bid/ask spreads, do you think more experienced traders were using candlesticks to their advantage? Of course they were. Now let me ask you a question. When I was trading Eastman Kodak, do you think I believed that I had some pretty advanced techniques at my command? You betcha! Was I making money? Sure I was! Could I have made more money if I had known about candlesticks? You bet!

Currently I use some pretty neat mathematical models to help me look at the markets. However, do you think that there are some other traders using techniques that I have no knowledge of? Of course there are. Can I make decent money trading commodities today using the techniques that I was using over 20 years ago? Sure I can. So what does this mean to you as a trader? What it means is that you must develop a way to see the price movement that you can relate to, in a very intimate and personal way. You must devise a model that allows you to determine if the market has continuity of bullish or bearish thought. Some of you are saying, "Great, just tell me what or how you can determine this!" Let me see if I can elaborate on it so that you can have a breakthrough experience.

What is a market? It is simply two individuals agreeing to make a transaction at a certain price. If you can imagine a wheat auction taking place with farmers and bakers present we can better understand how a market works. If the auction has not yet started, we will be unable to determine what the continuity of thought is in this instant of time. Once the auction starts and the first transaction takes place, we are still unable to determine what the continuity of thought is. All we know for sure is that we have a market as the farmer agreed to sell and the baker agreed to buy at a certain price. The farmer thinks the price will be lower in the future, and the baker thinks it will be higher. Now let us say that there is a second trade, and the price remains the same. Can we tell what the overall continuity of thought is now? Yes we can. The continuity of thought is that the supply meets the demand. We can say this because the price did not move. In other words, the expectations of the bullish bakers are being equally met by the bearish farmers.

Now there is a third trade, and the price goes up a little. What made it go up? Well, the expectations of the farmers might have changed so that they now think a drought could be coming. Consequently they will not sell at the lower price. However, perhaps the bakers thought that a drought was coming and decided to stock up before it actually arrived, driving up the prices. A third possibility is that the bakers had (or were expecting) a huge increase in demand, requiring more wheat. A fifth possibility is that the farmers discovered some of their crops had blight, reducing the supply in the near future. There could be a huge variety of reasons to make the price go up or down. As a speculator, could you know all the possible reasons that the price went up? Probably not.

Is it important to know all the reasons? Probably not. What is important is to determine what the continuity of thought is in the instant of time you are trading. What is an "instant of time"? Easy, it is the time period that you are focusing all your attention on. For example, if you are using end-of-day data, then the instant of time you are focusing on is daily. Can we tell what the continuity of thought is when the price of wheat went up? Of course. The continuity of thought is that wheat is going up, that the bulls are stronger than the bears. Can we make money knowing this? You bet! Is it this easy? Yes, and no. It is this easy if you have mastery of your virtues and vices. It is impossible if you are only beginning to comprehend how vitally important it is to have mastery of these character traits.

Now many of you are saying that there is no way it is this simple, and I am going to tell you that it is, provided your virtues, beliefs, and vices are mastered. Can you define the variations of trend that a market can exhibit? There are up trends, down trends, sideways to up trends, and sideways to down trends. That is it, there are no more price actions a market can exhibit than those four trends.

- Up trends are more commonly called a bull market. It is a market in which the continuity of bullish thought is in control. It is a market that the bulls are firmly in charge of, with the bears in total disarray.

- Sideways to up trends are more commonly called a sideways market (for those traders who are unable to see that there is a bullish basis). It is a market in which the continuity of thought is still up; however, the bears are expressing their strength. It is a market in which the bulls are starting to lose or gain control, and the bears are no longer in total disarray.

- Sideways to down trend are also more commonly called a sideways market (for those traders who are unable to see there is a bearish basis). It is a market in which the continuity of thought is still down; however, the bears are in charge and the bulls are expressing their strength. In this market the bears are starting to lose or gain control, and the bulls are no longer in total disarray.

- Down trends are more commonly called a bear market. It is a market in which the continuity of bearish thought is in control. It is a market that the bears are firmly in charge of, with the bulls in total disarray.

The more distinctions you can make about market behavior, the more successful you will be as a trader.

So the question rapidly becomes: How do you determine what the continuity of thought is? How do you make the distinction about what operating mode the market is in? I will answer this question in a minute. I would like first to tell you a few simple truths (beliefs of mine) about the different trending modes.

Let me start with a bull trend. I think the human psyche likes the idea of being a bull. It seems so logical to buy something and then sell it at a later date for a profit. Most beginning traders tend to establish long positions more readily than short positions. In a bull market the bulls are firmly in charge, and the bears are in total disarray. This means that a bull market will exhibit certain consistent characteristics. As you do your research you will observe certain characteristics that lead you to the conclusion that it is a bull market. Like an 800-pound male deer, a bull (market) will leave certain *droppings and hints* that it is present.

If you are an outdoor-type person you no doubt know what deer droppings look like, and you have also observed how the male deer marks certain trees by rubbing off bark with the velvet on his antlers. In the same way, a bull market will leave certain signs behind that you are witnessing a bull market. Deer climbing a mountain will never make a straight path to the summit. The deer will make frequent stops (hesitations), and retrace part of the upward journey (retracements) before resuming their climb to the summit. The critical thing to remember is that when the deer weaken, and retrace part of the upward path, they will often retreat to a lower pinnacle that they previously climbed, and will very rarely retreat beyond their last resting place in the previous valley. A deer will continue to climb the mountain looking for a cooler meadow to rest and eat in to escape the summer heat. The deer will start back down the mountain only if a bear chases him down—after all, bears like those very same meadows. Another reason a deer will go back down the hill is to find shelter in case of an approaching storm.

If the bear does in fact show up and chases the deer down the mountain, the bear will exhibit similar characteristics. The interesting thing is what transpires when both the deer and the bear co-exist on the same mountainside. In this case, one or the other will be slightly dominant, and although it will appear that they are moving sideways, they will in fact be moving up or down slightly. I suspect the reason that the bear doesn't chase the deer away, or vice versa, is that they are both being lazy, or they aren't certain who should be on the mountainside. It is easy to tell who has the edge, however, by observing which animal gets to eat and sleep in its preferred spot.

In other words, without the outdoorsy vernacular, in a bull market what was resistance for the bulls will often become support for the bulls upon any retracement. Should the bulls retrace past their previous resistance level, they will rarely go past a previous support area. However, should a bear market show up strong enough to spook the bulls, then previous areas that should have been support will fail. This is one of the first signs of a trend change.

When bears are in charge of the market, they will often retrace to a price level that was their former resistance level, and will rarely go past a former support area. Again, if the bears are unable to defend a former resistance area and then fail to defend a price that was support, they are weakening. Many novice traders think only of price as having support or resistance levels, when in actuality an indicator can also develop support of resistance levels. Figure 16-1 shows the bull/bear perspective from either a price or RSI perspective.

FIGURE 16-1   Bull/Bear Perspective

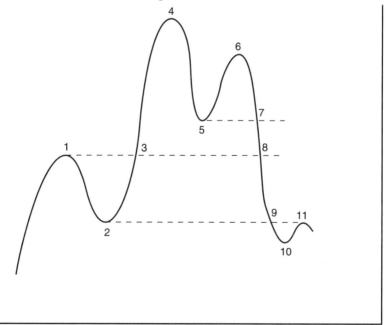

Time

The Bulls' Perspective

1. Bulls are getting tired, and they are experiencing some resistance for higher prices. This could be because there are not enough buyers or because the sellers (bears) are stronger.
2. Bulls find support.
3. Bulls overcome old resistance, which becomes support for the bulls.
4. Bulls advance to new high, before encountering new resistance, or overextending themselves.
5. Bulls retreat to a new support level, which is at or above points 1, 2, and 3.
6. Bulls encounter new resistance, where there was none previously; there are not enough bulls to push prices higher.
7. Bulls retreat again and obtain no support from other bulls that previously found support at point 5. The bulls may be in trouble.
8. Bulls retreat even lower, and still are not obtaining any support. Since this was a former resistance level that was overcome at point 3, there should be some support here. The bulls are definitely in trouble.
9. Bulls are in full-scale retreat, and find no support. The bulls have probably lost the upper hand.
10. At last the bulls find some support. In all probability the reason they do is that the bears got tired, or the bears became overextended.
11. Bulls manage to rally into new resistance, which was their former support. Without a doubt the continuity of bullish thought has been lost.

The Bears' Perspective

1. Bears wake up, and make this a support level.
2. Bears advance prices lower. Encountering resistance for lower prices, they could also be overextended.
3. Bears are unable to prevent the bulls from negating their former support level at point 1. The bears may be in trouble.
4. Bears find support among themselves to prevent higher prices, or the bulls are too few or tired to push higher.
5. Bears are able to push prices lower, encountering resistance by the bulls.
6. Bears find new support, lower than the support level at point 4. The bears are starting to assert their strength.

7.   Bears push prices lower, overcoming a price area that was their former resistance level, which now becomes their new support area.

8.   Bears push prices past an old resistance level of point 3 (which was also a former support level, point 1).

9.   Bears continue to encounter no resistance from the bulls at what was a major resistance level for the bears.

10. Bears at last encounter resistance, or it could be that the bears just got tired and overextended themselves. This is similar to the bulls encountering resistance at point 4.

11. Bears find support at this level, which coincides with their former resistance level, point 2. The continuity of thought is bearish.

If the market is experiencing continuity of bullish thought, then it is a bull market. It will be broken when enough traders perceive that the bulls are no longer the stronger force. Likewise, a bear market will be broken when enough traders perceive that the bears are no longer the stronger force.

A market that is sideways to up in trend will exhibit more characteristics of an up market than a down market. I am not being intentionally vague; however, it is a difficult trend to clearly identify. Shortly I will tell you how to use your computer to help define a sideways up or sideways down market. For now I can say only that if you draw a trend line off the peaks, and another trend line off the lows, the slope of the trend lines will be slightly up.

Whenever you see a market that is seemingly moving in a sideways channel, it will still have a predilection to be trending up or down. Often this is derived from the operating mode that the market was in prior to entering a sideways channel. There will always be a predilection tending to tip the trend in one direction or the other.

The important point I have been building to is this: When you are able to make the distinctions to identify the characteristics of the four operating modes, it is an easy matter to determine if you want to go long or short, or stay out of the market. When you have determined what mode the market is currently in and then a characteristic of that mode is violated, the market is telling you that the current trend is, or could be, about to change. Likewise when that characteristic is respected, then once again you are being told by the market that the trend, and its continuity of thought, is probably valid.

You absolutely must make yourself sensitive to what the continuity of thought is in each market that you are following.

In the previous examples I used support and resistance price areas as an example of a bull or bear market. Even though they are simple, I still use them extensively to this very day. Yes, I do have more precise indications of what characteristics each of the four trends should and should not exhibit. However, the point is that I have internalized these characteristics into my beliefs and references. As you begin developing your strategy on the basis of studies of different resources, you will begin to internalize these characteristics into your beliefs.

For example, my brother Frank makes extensive use of trend lines. He can tell you exactly what trend lines a bull market should respect—points that, if violated, will indicate either that the bull move is in trouble or that it is getting ready to accelerate up. There are more ways to draw trend lines than there are fish in the ocean. Frank, however, knows exactly how to draw *his* trend lines, because of his research, studies, and experience. While he and I disagree on how to draw a "proper" trend line, both of our approaches work. We both have a set of tools that we prefer to use because we have the certainty that they will work for us. We have the confidence that they are valid, and this gives us the courage to consistently use them. They help our intuition and allow us to remain persistent in applying our integrity to the trading environment. We remain flexible in looking at new methods.

Here, then, is the cornerstone of all my technical analysis. I use these strategies to this day when looking at a market to decide if it justifies more attention. While they may or may not seem simple, let me assure you that when you are trading a 21-tick chart in a fast bond market, simplicity is critical for effectiveness!

Over the years, friends who are traders have asked me how I can so quickly determine a trend when looking at a chart. The answer, I suspect, is experience to some degree. However, the experience is based on one fundamental indicator that I faithfully use every day. That indicator is the Relative Strength Index (RSI), as developed by J. Welles Wilder, Jr. and presented in his 1978 book *New Concepts in Technical Trading Systems.* Welles Wilder developed it for pork bellies, and it is my belief that a valid indicator will work in all markets, and in all time periods. I was fortunate to have studied with Andrew Cardwell, Jr., CTA, who has realized, through intense research, that there is much more the RSI can offer.

The fact that an indicator works in all time periods is important. I believe that if an indicator is valid, it will work in all time frames, from a tick chart to a monthly chart. The RSI is used:

- To analyze trends
- To spot trend changes
- To set price objectives

The RSI is a momentum-derived oscillator that is very popular among futures traders, and some stock traders. Typically oscillators based on momentum or price differences will have a problem when there are erratic and sharp price movements within the time period under consideration. When a big advance or decline is finally dropped from the time period used by the momentum oscillator, it will cause the oscillator to show a movement even if in actuality there is little price movement.

Suppose you are using a simple 10-period rate-of-change (ROC) indicator and 10 days ago there was a huge move (up or down). However, yesterday and today the price barely changed. Consequently the ROC indicator will barely change today from yesterday. Now let us go forward one day, and once again the price barely changes. You would think that the oscillator would also change just a little. In reality the oscillator will change a lot, since the huge move made (now) 11 days ago has been dropped from the mathematical calculation.

The RSI will dampen or smooth out these distortions. In addition, a typical momentum indicator is not contained within a predefined vertical range. Hence you must constantly refer to past history when comparing past highs or lows, in order to determine oversold or overbought conditions. Again the RSI solves this problem, since the indicator is contained within a vertical range of 0 to 100.

Many books on technical analysis use a 9- or 14-period look-back to perform the RSI calculations. The longer the time period, the less sensitive the oscillator becomes, and the smaller its amplitude. I like the RSI with a time period of 14, because it works best for me and, as strange as it may sound, is half the lunar cycle. The rest of this discussion on RSI levels will use the 14-period look-back, regardless of whether we are looking at hourly charts or monthly charts. I use the 14-period look-back on all markets over all time periods, including the 5-minute bar chart. In order to gain more sensitivity, some traders will use the shorter 9-period look-back.

For the RSI formula to give valid results, you want to have at least 90 days (or periods) of data. Should you have fewer than 90 periods, the results given by the RSI formula will not be accurate for trend analysis. I prefer to have at least 200 periods of data when looking at any chart. In other words, if I am trading off of a 5-minute chart (each bar represents 5 minutes), I want to have at least 200 bars or 1000 minutes of data.

Books on technical analysis typically state that any movement above 70 on the RSI is overbought, while any movement under 30 is oversold. An important fact to remember is that any oscillator (the RSI included) in a strongly trending market will become either oversold in a bear market or overbought in a bull market. The indicator can remain oversold or over-bought for quite a while.

According to Wilder, the greatest value of the RSI is in pointing out a divergence between the RSI and price. As Figure 16-2 shows, a bullish divergence (or as he calls it a bottom failure swing) occurs when the price makes a low while the RSI (when under 30) fails to make a new low. This can be seen at point *c,* where the RSI value is higher than at point *a,* while the price is lower. When the RSI proceeds to exceed the previous RSI peak (at point *b*), a short-term buy signal is generated according to Wilder. The opposite applies to a bearish divergence, and is considered a short-term selling opportunity. In Figure 16-3, we can see how 70 acts as resistance and 30 acts as support. The typical trader uses the RSI to identify a bearish divergence when the RSI is over 70, and a bullish divergence when the RSI is under 30.

That pretty much sums up public knowledge about the RSI. However, what the average trader comprehends is a small part of the overall picture,

FIGURE 16-2   Bullish Divergence

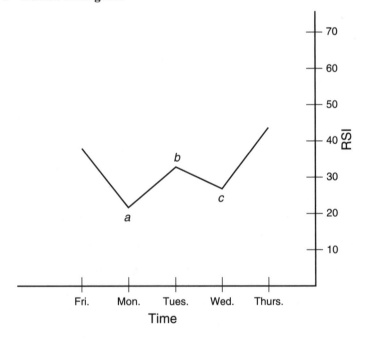

Key:

a Price is at 100, RSI is at 22

b Price is at 102, RSI is at 32

c Price is at 98, RSI is at 27

FIGURE 16-3   Wilder's RSI Chart

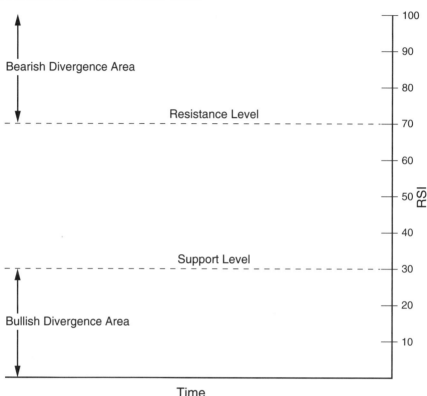

as Andrew Cardwell Jr. showed. What most traders do not realize is that the RSI range effectively shifts in an up trend so that 80 becomes overbought. This necessitates that the support level also shift upward. Inversely, in a bear market the oversold level shifts down to 20, with the resistance level in a bear market also shifting downward.

Up-trending markets typically find support at the 40 level with effective resistance at the 80 level. Down-trending markets find resistance at 60 with effective support at the 20 level. Often one of the first indications that the trend has shifted from a bear trend to a possible bull market is that the RSI, which previously was respecting the 60 level, will rally up to 70 or higher. When the inevitable decline arrives, the RSI will respect the 40 level, and then rally.

A *range shift* occurs when the RSI value violates a level that had been acting as support or resistance. The RSI then proceeds to start respecting a new support or resistance level. In other words, if the market has been trending up, then the RSI values have been oscillating within the 80/40 range. The bulls will find a reason to get long every time the RSI value approaches the 40 level. Should the bulls fail to buy when the RSI value declines to the 40 level, and the RSI value declines to, say, 30 before turning back up, a range shift has probably taken place. Confirmation of such a range shift occurs when the RSI value rallies and fails to go over the 60 level before dropping. When the RSI violates the 40 level, it is often the first indication that the trend is changing. The reason that typically the first indication comes with the range shift is because the RSI is a momentum oscillator. The interesting thing about momentum oscillators is that they *lead* price action. In other words, momentum, since it measures the rate (or speed) that prices are changing, will always begin to weaken before the price weakens. So in an up trend, momentum will quit moving up while prices continue to move higher.

As shown in Figure 16-4, in an 80/40 range the RSI will oscillate between 80 and 40—a strong indication of a bull market! Likewise, in a 60/20 range the RSI will oscillate between 60 and 20—a strong indication of a bear market! When I look at a chart of a commodity or stock I always look at the RSI. I want to see what range it is in—this is the first technical indication of the trend. It should be confirming what the price action is telling me. The RSI will also find resistance or support at previous tops or bottoms in the RSI itself. Old resistance points could become new resistance points and, if broken, a new support level upon a retracement. Likewise, old support levels could prove to be effective support again and, if broken, will prove to be effective resistance. In Figure 16-5, we see how bonds rallied from a low of 118 to 135 over a period of 6 months while the RSI remained above 40. We can also see how in early July the RSI rallied (point g), and again in early August (point h) that became support when the RSI declined in September. Point i found support at what was resistance (point g), and point j found support at point h, a former resistance level.

You always want to watch for former support and resistance levels, in both the price chart and the RSI chart. My trading platform allows me to type notes, prices, and fundamental events directly onto my price chart. Then every day when I reload, I see all my notes right there on the chart. Every chart I look at always has the price action (displayed as candlesticks) in the top part of the screen and an RSI chart directly under it. I then type the price onto the RSI chart at every point where the RSI reversed itself. In this manner I can look at my RSI chart and see the price where the RSI found effective resistance and support. I can also see what level the RSI itself found effective resistance and support. In a trending bull market, the price and the RSI charts will both show that what was

FIGURE 16-4   Cardwell's RSI Chart

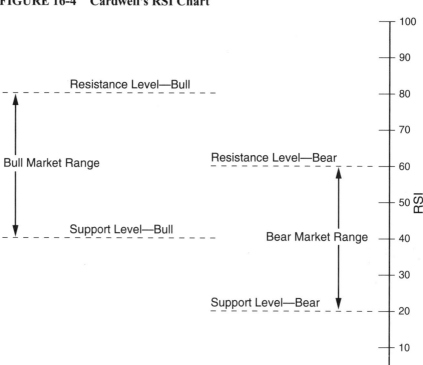

a resistance level several days or weeks ago is now becoming support. This is indicative of an up-trending market.

Just as with a price chart, you can draw trend lines and see patterns develop on an RSI chart. On a price chart if you draw a trend line based on three higher bottoms, you can expect support to develop any time the price declines to the trend line a fourth time. Should the price continue to decline through this trend line, you will often get a retest of that trend line as the bulls attempt to pierce the line, this time from underneath. This retest from under the former bullish trend line, which was acting as support and is now acting as resistance, is a typical distinction of a bear market. This same principle applies to the RSI; a violation of a proven trend line on the RSI chart will often occur prior to a violation of a trend line on a price chart.

Double tops and bottoms, symmetrical triangles, bullish falling wedges, bearish rising wedges, and descending and ascending triangles can all be found on an RSI chart, and all are valid. Likewise you can expect to

FIGURE 16-5   Trend Determination

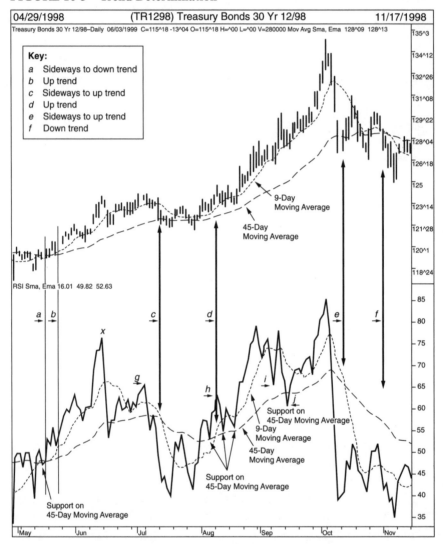

see the RSI oscillator value after a rally make a retracement of 38, 50, or 61 percent—pretty interesting stuff! I will keep my eye open for these patterns to emerge, and use them in my analysis. The most common pattern I find is a symmetrical triangle. I have found that the longer the RSI stays within the triangle the more violent the breakout becomes.

It is interesting that the RSI is contained between 0 and 100—the same as the bullish consensus figures. Another way to perceive the RSI numbers

FIGURE 16-6   Bearish Divergence

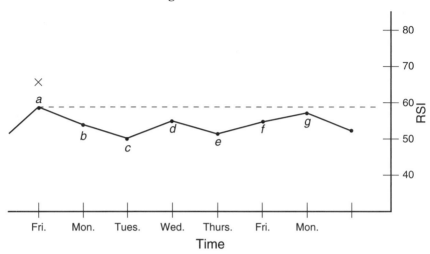

Key:

a   Price is at 123.0, RSI is at 58.0
b   Price is at 121.0, RSI is at 54.0
c   Price is at 119.0, RSI is at 49.0
d   Price is at 120.0, RSI is at 56.0
e   Price is at 119.5, RSI is at 52.0
f   Price is at 121.5, RSI is at 55.0
g   Price is at 125.0, RSI is at 57.0

is that when the RSI is at 60, there is a 40 percent chance that the RSI will continue up. If the oscillator value is at 81, there is only a 19 percent chance that it could continue on up. To date, I have never seen a market in which the bulls were able to get the RSI much above 90. It is important to remember that in a strongly up-trending market a momentum oscillator will become overbought (above 70) or oversold (under 30) and will remain over-bought/oversold while prices continue much higher/lower. Typically when the RSI or any momentum oscillator becomes overextended, any slight price movement in the opposite direction of the primary trend will be magnified by the oscillator, while any price movement in the original direction of the primary trend is suppressed. Typically this type of price or momentum movement creates a divergence between the behavior of price versus RSI. This is easily seen in Figure 16-5 in early June. Bonds made a new high with the RSI rallying to just under 80 (point *x*). Fourteen days later the price once again was at the same level as previously, yet the RSI value (point *g*) was under 70. Subsequently, price declined into mid-July retracing a percentage of the prior rally from May to June. However, the RSI retraced almost the entire prior rally in the RSI. We see this behavior once again at points *g* and *h,* where the price that coincides with point *h* is above the price that coincides with point *g,* yet the RSI value is lower. When we see this behavior we call it a divergence. A divergence occurs when the momentum oscillator is not reflecting price action. In other words, price will make a higher high, yet the momentum oscillator will not exceed its previous high. This is called a bearish divergence. Inversely, whenever the price makes a new low yet the momentum oscillator fails to exceed its previous low, we are seeing a bullish divergence. In Figure 16-2, we see a bullish divergence, and in Figure 16-6, we see a bearish divergence.

The reason it is called either bearish or bullish is because the price will typically sell off after a bearish divergence is formed and rally after a bullish divergence is made. Unfortunately, the majority of traders unconsciously associate a bearish divergence with a bear market and a bullish divergence with a bull market. This association is totally false. An important clue about the market direction is to constantly be looking for a divergence.

Now what I am about to say next will cause traders with any rudimentary knowledge of divergences to fry a few brain cells and have smoke come out of their ears! Whenever I see a bearish divergence I immediately start thinking that we are in, or about to enter into, a bull market! Whenever I see a bullish divergence I start thinking that we are in, or about to enter into, a bear market! Yes I know that this flies in the face of what all the textbooks say.

The important point is that in the vast majority of cases repeated bearish divergences occur only in an up-trending market, and bullish divergences repeatedly occur in a bearish market. If you find this hard to accept then get a chart of the Japanese yen and start looking at what the RSI did from July 1995 to August 1998. You will be hard-pressed to find a bearish divergence in the daily chart, and there is no bearish divergence in the weekly chart covering a period of 3 years. In Figure 16-5 from the rally commencing in May to October there is no bull divergence—only bear divergences! Then in late October the RSI did make a bull divergence—but what did the price do? This is the third thing I look at; it is one of my favorite tools. Since the vast majority of traders lose their money, since most traders will sell a bearish divergence, and since most traders are bearish when they are short, I will be waiting to buy!

Divergences are associated with any momentum-based indicator. They typically show up at the momentum high or low. When a bull market is overbought, there is a loss of momentum, then a downward correction in price, but not necessarily a trend change. In other words, when a bearish divergence occurs, the market is telling you that it is currently overbought or overextended and that you may want to take partial profits on your long position, since the price may be about to take a price detour. It is not telling you to get short!

A divergence takes a certain number of time periods to form. The *strength of a divergence* is based on this period of time. The probability is that the price will retrace some of its prior move increases as the strength of the divergence increases. A divergence that has a period of 5 will be a lot stronger than a 20-period divergence. Here's how to calculate the period of a divergence. Let's say that prices have been advancing (on a daily chart) over the past few weeks, and the price and the RSI are both making new highs, as we can see in Figure 16-6. For the next two days the price and the RSI both drop (points *b* and *c*), then the price and the RSI reverse and rally (point *d*) for one day followed by a drop in price and the RSI (point *e*). This decline is followed by a two-day rally (points *f* and *g*). At the close of the second day (point *g*) of this short rally, the price is higher than it was six days earlier (point *a*), yet the RSI is under its previous peak. This is a six-day bearish divergence. When looking at a chart, place an X at the RSI high (point *a*), then start counting the number of days it took for the RSI to "hook" over and drop. You then get the number of days that the divergence signal took to form. This is important to know, since a six-day divergence is usually indicative of a detour in price. The longer-period divergences usually indicate a lower probability of a price detour coming. The most powerful divergence is a 2- or 3-period divergence. In the overall context of using the RSI in trading, the divergence signals are relatively minor. I like using divergence to give me a clue of what the overall trend is and where to take partial profits in a multiple-contract position.

Another tool I use to indicate trend is the old workhorse of technicians, moving averages. Moving averages are valuable, since they remove the volatility from the calculations. By using a moving average based on a 14-period RSI, you are effectively removing the volatility of the last 14 days, yielding a smoother signal. I like using a 9-period simple moving average, and a 45-period weighted moving average. I calculate a simple 9-period moving average and a 45-period weighted moving average on the closing price and on the RSI value. This results in four moving averages, and by using them together, I can confirm the trend. In this way I can quickly determine which of the four operating modes the market is in. Figure 16-5 shows how the different moving averages interact with each other.

1.   When the 9-period moving average based on price is above its respective 45-period moving average, and the 9-period moving average based on the RSI is above the 45-period based on RSI, the trend is UP (at points *b* and *d* in Figure 16-5).

2.   When the 9-period moving average based on price is below its respec-
     tive 45-period moving average, and the 9-period moving average based
     on the RSI is below the 45-period on RSI, the trend is DOWN (at points
     f and prior to point *a* in Figure 16-15).
3.   When the 9-period moving average based on price is above its
     respective 45-period moving average, and the 9-period moving aver-
     age based on the RSI is below the 45-period on RSI, the trend is
     SIDEWAYS TO UP (at points *a* and *c* in Figure 16-5).
4.   When the 9-period moving average based on price is below its
     respective 45-period moving average, and the 9-period moving aver-
     age based on the RSI is above the 45-period on RSI, the trend is
     SIDEWAYS TO DOWN (at points *c* and *e* in Figure 16-5).

Since the RSI is a momentum-derived oscillator and since momentum
often leads price, the 9-period moving average on the RSI will cross its
respective 45-period moving average, before the 9-period on price will cross
its respective 45-period moving average. I place more emphasis on the moving averages based on price. By staying aware of how the moving averages
are behaving, you will remain focused on the overall trend. When I talk to
another trader, I often say that the moving average on price is positive, the
implication being that the short-term (9) moving average is above the long-
term (45) moving average. The largest moves come when both moving averages head in the same direction, as can be seen in Figure 16-5 at points *b* to *c*
and *d* to *e*.

One last thought on moving averages. The 45-period moving average
will often prove to be support or resistance for the price, or the RSI. For
example, a bullish market may retrace to its respective 45-period moving
average (price and/or RSI), and then bounce off it, as can be seen in Figure
16-5. This is another sign of what the trend actually is, and in this case it indicates that the bulls are using the 45-period moving average as a support level
to get long.

When I am determining what the trend is, I ask myself the following
questions:

1.   What is the RSI range? Has there been a range shift?
2.   Is the market respecting the support and resistance areas of the domi-
     nant force, or is the market violating them and reversing their roles?
3.   Have we broken an important trend line in the price or RSI chart?
4.   What types of divergences are present?
5.   What are the moving averages attempting to tell us?

This may or may not be basic information to you. I still use these fundamental techniques when analyzing the markets. I want to quickly determine what trend the market I am looking at is presently exhibiting.

As you develop your own methodology in determining what the trend is, it is important to make sure that your overall methodology works in all time frames. Although a 5-minute chart of the S&P will exhibit certain characteristics that will not be seen on a monthly chart, the overall characteristics will be similar. Your goal is to be able to quickly and efficiently determine what the continuity of thought is in the particular market that you are looking at. At this point you are attempting to determine, not when or at what price to enter the market, just what operating mode it is in at this point in time.

Remember that once you can accurately and quickly determine what mode the market is in, you have determined only what the trend *has* been. You are looking at past information. You have determined what the market has been doing, what the continuity of thought *has been*. To paraphrase Sir Isaac Newton, unless there is a change in continuity of thought to act upon a market, then that market will continue in the direction it was originally heading. Unfortunately, the continuity of thought could change instantly.

This is where many novice traders make a fatal error. After much research they arrive at a point that they are certain they can look at a chart using their methodology and state that "this is a bear market." So they promptly go short, and then the very next day the continuity of thought that the market had is broken, and the market rallies. Now their ego gets involved and they stay with the trade. As the market rallies, they insist that it is a bear market and that they will eventually be vindicated—that is, until they can no longer meet the margin call, or stand the pain, and have to exit their losing trade.

When determining the continuity of thought using yesterday's data, always keep in mind that you are looking at past, old, stagnant information. Although the market is influenced by yesterday's price action, what the continuity of thought is right now will always be reflected in what the market is doing right now! Your goal is always to determine what the continuity of thought is for the time period you are trading in, and to be ready to exit the trade at the first indication of trouble. What the market did today (or the current period if you are not trading daily charts) will give an indication of what it *might* be doing tomorrow. By entering the market when its direction *right now* agrees with your perception of what the market was doing previously, you are increasing the probability that you will be able to profit from the *continued* direction of the market.

Determining the trend of the market is critically important for your long-term success. However, just because the market was in a particular trend in the previous period does not guarantee the market will continue in that direction—only the probability of its doing so.

17

ENTRY AND EXIT STRATEGIES

Trends tend to persist . . . until they don't. And that's why God made stops.

—FRANK GRETZ

Safety and surety lie only in buying after a market has risen sufficiently from its bottom to show that its previous troubles are past, and in selling before the rise has become a matter of mere foam that, in the natural order of things, must presently vanish. And for the bear it means that the time to sell is after a market has definitely turned downward from a hysterical top, and the time to cover is before hysteria has produced an unjustifiably low bottom.

—BERNARD E. "SELL 'EM BEN" SMITH

O NCE YOU HAVE defined what continuity of thought the market is reflecting, you must decide how to profit from this knowledge. As we know, every excellent trader has different rules and/or procedures to enter or exit the market. Your goal at this time is to determine what methodology you want to use to enter or exit, and then use it consistently.

The exact method you decide to use will relate to how you determine what the operating mode of the market is, how you define risk, your beliefs, and your money management rules. There are many different entry techniques you could use, and they all relate to your risk tolerance.

Suppose a trader has come to the conclusion that the market is, or is about to, demonstrate a strong continuity of bullish thought. Here is a *partial* list of strategies the trader could use to get long:

1. Waiting for a retracement in price:
   A. To a bullish trend line.
   B. To a certain percentage of the previous move.
   C. To retest a previous resistance area.
   D. To retest a previous support area.
   E. For a certain price or mathematical formula behavior to occur, signifying an end to that retracement.
2. Waiting for the price to continue up and:
   A. To go through a price that has been mathematically calculated.
   B. To go up (break through) through a previous price that previously acted as support or resistance in a declining market.
3. Waiting for a mathematically derived study to do something.
4. Getting long as soon as the continuity of bearish thought has been broken.
5. Getting long as soon as the realization that the technicals and the fundamentals are in alignment—that is, they both have a continuity of bullish thought.

There are some huge variations that encompass the above reasons for going long. It is beyond the intention of this book to go into detail on all the possible variations. The critical fact is that you must come up with a set of rules that you trust to get you into a bull move every single time. In all probability when you are done you will be able to fit your exact technique into one of the above classifications.

Can you have different entry techniques for getting long? Sure you can, provided you have an associated set of rules (beliefs) for each different entry technique. You must be able to say that you went long because of this, this, and this reason. By having exact rules on what made you enter the trade, you will be able over time to reexamine the underlying logic of these rules and determine if the methodology is profitable. Note that we do not care if our reasons are logical (although that would be nice), only that they are quantifiable and repeatable, can be consistently applied, and are profitable.

For example, you could have one set of rules to get long when the continuity of thought is very strong in a trending market. Another set of rules could be used when the trend is sideways (up-down), and yet another set of rules could apply when the continuity of thought of the dominant force has just been shattered! However, it is absolutely imperative that your rules be rooted on quantifiable actions of the market, and that they occur fairly frequently.

When you are starting out designing your entry rules, you must keep in mind what your exit rules will or might be. What do you believe is more important: your entry price or exit price? Most experienced traders will put more emphasis into developing rules to exit a trade. This is because when you are flat, and only looking at a market, your rational mind is not being unduly influenced by your emotional mind. Hopefully you are able to see the market as it is; however, as soon as you enter into the trade your emotional mind will begin to unduly influence your perceptions and logical abilities. When a soldier is in the heat of battle, his life will often depend on the cold, detached, unemotional abilities of his general. Your exit rules will be a major defense against your emotional feelings and ego.

The best way to develop your entry and exit rules is to define your overall trading strategy. Go back and reread the possible strategies on going long and ask yourself *why* you would want to adopt each of those strategies. Do this now before reading any more; there are no right or wrong answers.

Here are a few beliefs traders might have on why they want to buy at a price higher than it currently is:

1.   By continuing higher, the market has demonstrated that it is willing to go higher.

2.   By waiting till a higher price has been accomplished, the market is indicating that it will probably continue higher.

3.   By waiting for the bulls to rally prices above a price level that the bears should have defended, the market is indicating that the bulls are in firm command.

Now here are a few beliefs traders might have on why they would rather wait for a retracement in price or in a mathematical formula:

1. By waiting for a retest of a valid trend line, the trader could use a small stop. The trend line has already demonstrated its power to rally prices *in the past.*

2. By waiting for a percentage retracement, the trader is acknowledging that some market moves will retrace 33, 50, or 66 percent, and by waiting the trader will be going long at a much better price that may allow for a tighter stop.

3. By waiting for a retest of a previous resistance or support price level, the trader is acknowledging the significance of how what was resistance for the bulls should now be support, or previous bullish support should remain support, provided that the continuity of thought is still up. Here too, tighter stops may be used.

4. By waiting for the retracement, and then for the *price* or a *mathematical formula* to behave in a certain manner, the trader can look for a particular pattern that in the past has represented the resumption of the bull move. The stop order can then be placed closer to the entry price.

The reason that traders wait for their mathematically based study or program to do something before they enter is that they have been able to identify a pattern through their math or program, allowing them to enter into a trade with the best *probability* that the trade is going to work.

Getting long as soon as the continuity of bearish thought has been broken allows the trader to get into a bull move before the rest of the traders have realized the continuity of thought has been broken. Getting long when the realization that the technical and the fundamentals are in alignment allows the trader to be fairly certain that the bull market will continue. It means that the trader will not be chopped to death—that is, both the technical and fundamental traders share the belief that the bulls are or will be the dominant force.

You need to understand that there is no ideal way to enter the market. There is an ideal way for *you* to enter the market. Only you can determine what that method is. Whatever method you use to enter into a trade, you must be comfortable with the underlying reason that you are entering in that manner, and you must be able to make it quantifiable.

Remember, there is no holy grail. Your responsibility to yourself is to define how you see the market, how you want to enter the market, what has to happen for you to acknowledge that your trade isn't working as you had planned, and what has to happen for you to exit a trade. You will develop a unique perspective on how the market works as you learn about the market, study the different technical and fundamental tools available, and develop your methodology to determine the price action, how you enter and exit a trade, and what type of risk parameters you use.

TRADING AS METAPHOR

A trader's overall perspective on how the market works is often best viewed in metaphoric terms that compare trading with something else. A metaphor allows you to integrate your conscious, and unconscious beliefs into one harmonious reality. A metaphor can be empowering, helping you in your trading efforts, or it can be negative and prevent you from seeing the market effectively. To determine your metaphor for trading finish this sentence: "Trading is...."

"Trading is a battle" is a metaphor that can carry many different emotional feelings. If trading is a battle, does it also mean that if you are not careful you can be killed? Does it mean that a losing trade is cause for great concern? Does it mean that if you are not careful you could lose your financial life? Does it mean that trading is only a battle—not the war? Does it mean all these things or none of them? Which ones carry the most intense feelings? Which ones enable the trader to respond out of virtue?

"Trading is a three-dimensional chess game" is a metaphor that *probably* has less negative emotional intensity than "Trading is a battle." "Trading is like dancing a waltz" is yet another metaphor with probably even less negative emotional energy. How might your trading be affected if your metaphor for the markets was "Trading is like soaring with the eagles"?

It is impossible to tell, without delving into the rules, references, and values of the individual trader, if any of these metaphors is empowering or negative. However, we could say that in all probability a trader who views the market as a battle will see trading far more seriously than a trader who sees the market as a dance. The importance of a metaphor is that it creates a reality for traders that allows them to enter into a trade with a certain amount of faith. In a strict sense there are no right or wrong metaphors. However, in a general sense there are negative or empowering metaphors. These metaphors will evolve as your perspective of the market expands into a functioning methodology.

Here are some metaphors from various traders to describe the markets:

"The markets are like two armies in a never-ending series of battles.
My job is to hitch a ride on the food truck of the stronger force."

"Trading is the ability to figure out what all the other traders are reading into the future."

"Every time I enter the market I feel like I just jumped into shark-
infested waters, and I am their lunch. For me to make money, all
my indicators have to be perfectly aligned."

"Trading is like a game of 'hide and seek' that children play. I wait
quietly and patiently for the market to present a profitable opportunity to come and play!"

Which metaphor do you think I heard from a trader who had lost
approximately $10,000 a day for the previous nine days, had wiped out
his trading account, and was wiring in money to meet the margin call?
Which trader has the best metaphor for trading? Which trader trades from
stress, and which one trades from a more relaxed viewpoint?

I mention metaphors because they influence your perception, and your
beliefs influence your metaphors. Metaphors influence how you decide to
enter into a trade. Some professional traders like to catch a market low,
others look at the chart and fundamental picture before getting into a
trade, others look only at fundamentals, others read only the tape, and
others look only at technicals. As you research the markets and begin to
figure out how you will determine what trend the market is in, you will
begin to develop your metaphor. As you find yourself explaining to others
how the market works, be aware of whether the metaphor you are using is
empowering or limiting. Your conscious mind gives you the ability to
decide if you will use a disempowering metaphor. The trader who had lost
money had a limiting metaphor. The hint that it was limiting was the seri-
ous negative connotation of sharks eating him and the fact that he said "all
my indicators have to be perfectly aligned." Using any form of the word
"perfect" sets you up to fail, since in the real world nothing is ever as perfect as it could possibly be, especially when you are using multiple indicators. Consequently the likelihood of having the discipline to wait for
everything to line up is rather remote. This trader has a very difficult time
entering the market. You would too if you thought you were jumping into
shark-infested waters!

Very rarely will you find a methodology that has multiple indicators
perfectly aligned. In many cases you will realize they were "almost" per-

fectly aligned only after they are no longer aligned, so now you are forced to enter the trade after the fact! I have found that if I use any metaphor that suggests I can somehow predict the price movement then I am creating stress and anxiety. Here is my extended metaphor for the market:

> The market is like the game of GO. Whereas the game of GO is played on a horizontal board of 19 vertical and horizontal lines, the market game is played in the space between my ears, on a vertical board of price and time. As in GO, where I play from the strength of my stones and intellect, I play the market from the strength of my beliefs and virtues, and the annihilation of my vices. I place my GO stone at a place on the board where it will create the best tactical advantage. I place my order to enter at a price and time that I have identified as a critical price for me to profit.

My metaphor is what allows me to trade effectively. Underlying my metaphor is a score of beliefs, references, and values. It allows me to enter and exit a trade with certainty and conviction. It took me a long time to create my metaphor, I did not set out to create it; it was created from the thousands of hours of research. Don't worry if you don't understand it. You must be a GO player to begin to fully understand the ramifications.

EXITS VERSUS STOPS

Pick up any book on technical analysis and look up "exit" and "stop" in the index. What you may discover is that there is a section on stops and none on exits, or a short paragraph devoted to exit strategy and a page devoted to stops. Why is this? Can we assume that because exit strategies are barely discussed they aren't important? Do you know the differences between getting stopped out and making a decision to exit?

All too often, traders devote all their energies to devising a methodology on how and when to get into a market. Then after hundreds if not thousands of research hours, they sit back and think they are finally done because they can positively identify a bull market, sideways to up, sideways to down, and a bear market. After a little reflection they figure that they had better develop some sort of exit strategy. Consequently they will spend a small amount of time on an exit strategy and then consider their work done.

Your exit strategy is critical to your financial survival. Your exit strategy will invariably be related to your entry strategy and your risk tolerance. For all too many traders the exit strategy is nonexistent, and is in fact the same as their stop placement strategy! I guess this is not too surprising, given the emphasis that technical books place on entry strategies. There is a huge difference between an exit strategy and a stop placement strategy.

An effective exit strategy will allow you to keep more profits than just allowing your trade to be stopped out with a trailing stop. Unfortunately, the vast majority of traders allow their profitable trades to be stopped out. What is the difference? An effective exit strategy requires active monitoring, and more work than it took to enter. In most cases a stop placement strategy is fairly automated. The reason the exit strategy takes more work is that when you are in a trade your disempowering beliefs are attempting to create emotions that distort your ability to perceive the market. It takes a conscious effort to overcome this.

Effective exit strategies incorporate valid reentry strategies.

Depending upon your trading methodology, you may want to exit the trade whenever the continuity of thought has been broken or has weakened. If you exit a trade because you think the continuity of thought has weakened, do you have a strategy to reenter the trade, or do you wait for another signal like the one that got you into the trade in the first place? The biggest hindrance to investing the time needed to devise an exit strategy is your ego. Many traders watch a market shoot up to the sun, and then watch it retrace all the way back down. Most traders fail to exit at the first sign of weakness, because they do not have a valid reentry technique. Most traders would rather allow their stop to take them out of the trade, because their belief structure has created some very powerful arguments for doing so. Your beliefs will create a whole lot of reasons not to exit the winning trade, even after you are fairly sure that the continuity of thought has been broken. The correct way to reenter a trade after the continuity of thought resumes is to have a different entry strategy that gets you back in immediately.

The important thing is to use a quantifiable methodology to determine if the market is weakening. You have to be able to identify exactly what caused you to think that the market was weakening. You must be able to do this because if you find yourself repeatedly exiting a winning trade, and then reentering at a more adverse price, you can take active steps to change how you identify a weakening of market consensus. *The market will always tell you when your methodology needs to be refined—by the red ink that you see.* This demands that you use pinpoint precision in determining the underlying reasons for making the trade. It also requires that you consistently use your perception and behave free of disempowering beliefs or vices. Only then will you be able to improve your methodology.

The challenge to exit strategies is that you are exiting a trade that has in the past demonstrated a strong continuity of thought about where it is heading. In every case the market will not climb to the sun or sink to the center of the earth without signs of hesitation. Every time the market expresses itself, there will be resistance by the opposing force, either immediately or eventually. If you devise a strategy that exits at the first sign of resistance, you might be getting out of your trades prematurely. Yet if you wait for a lot of resistance, you are probably leaving a lot of money on the table. In fact, your trailing stop could be just slightly lower than your exit price, if you wait for a lot of resistance.

Money management is covered in depth in the next chapter. However, your exit strategy and your stop strategies must mutually reinforce each other. You want to capture as much profit as possible while simultaneously reducing your exposure to loss.

The dilemma is that if we make our exit strategy too sensitive, we open ourselves to exiting a long-term trend prematurely. We may then be forced to reenter, adversely affecting our total profits. However, if we exit only when the trend clearly has changed, we will leave a lot of money on the table. Should the perceived trend we entered on turn out to be not that long and/or fail to move up or down significantly, we could exit the trade at a loss. The other challenge with waiting for the trend to change is that we have to allow the market so much room to retrace part of its move that our protective stop will remain at a price that, if hit, would result in a loss or a significant reduction of profits. So what is a trader supposed to do?

The answer that I have found is best demonstrated by example. Let us assume that I have a very simple methodology, based on weekly data, that uses the RSI and defines a bull trend as whenever a bearish divergence occurs, and a bear trend as whenever a bullish divergence occurs. I will go short on Monday's open, only after a bearish candlestick appears in the ensuing bear rally; when a bullish divergence is present, I will go long by reversing those rules. My exit strategy is to remain short until there is a bearish divergence, at which point I exit on the open on Monday of the following week. My stop loss is determined by finding the range of the week that made the bearish candlestick and dividing the range by 2. This value is then added to the open of Monday (where I got short); this then is my stop loss price.

Let's take an example that occurred a few years back and bring it into the present. Looking at a weekly yen chart, I see that on 2/9/96 there was a bullish divergence and on 2/23/96 there was a bearish candlestick indicating the rally was over. So I go short yen the following week on the open at 9576. Now that I am short I continue to examine a weekly chart to see if the trend is changing. Since I am also using the weekly chart to generate the exit strategy, I have to accept that I will leave a lot of money on the table, when the market changes direction.

What I have found in order for my exit strategy to keep more profits is that I need to go to a shorter time period. The next shorter time frame from weekly is daily (the common belief). I will continue to wait for the continuity of thought to change on a daily basis from bearish to bullish. Consequently I have to change my exit strategy to exit when there is a bearish divergence, on a daily chart. When it does change, I will now exit the short yen trade the next day. This was accomplished on 4/23/96 at a price of 9446, a $1625 gain.

Now after exiting the yen short I will focus my attention on two time frames: the weekly and the daily. I will go short if the weekly chart generates another short order. I will alternatively reenter the short yen trade, based on the daily chart, if it generates the same signal that the weekly chart generated previously (a bullish divergence and a bearish candlestick). In my example the weekly yen chart did not generate another sell signal. However, the daily chart on 6/11/96 had another bullish divergence; then on 6/20/96 there was a bearish candlestick following the bear rally at 9401. So I go short on the open the next day, 6/21/96, at 9354. My stop is based on the weekly chart, and I will now continue watching the weekly and the daily charts for my exit strategy to be exercised. It finally was. On 6/12/97 I exited following a bearish divergence at 8760, a $7425 profit.

This strategy of using a shorter time frame is not typically discussed in the vast majority of technical analysis books. This is a pity, because it is very effective. The purpose of this example is not to demonstrate some great methodology (it was profitable, but not that great), but to demonstrate how your methodology will be enhanced by deciding to use an exit strategy (with a reentry strategy) in conjunction with a stop strategy. Different time frames may be something that you want to consider. There is a significant amount of extra work required to do all the research involved in using different time frames. A lot of professional traders do not base their trading decisions on anything but one time frame; however, some use multiple time frames. A friend of mine in New York makes trades from a 5-dimensional representation of the market based on different time frames, ticks, and some fairly advanced math. The secret is that you must devise a methodology based upon the beliefs that you have faith in.

Interestingly, if the shorter time frame (in this example, daily) continues to exhibit a continuity of thought indicative of a bull market, then I will
be ready to go long when the time frame I was using (weekly) generates a
buy signal according to my methodology.

I should stress an important point about using multiple time frames.
There are advantages and disadvantages to all time frames. Monthly and
weekly charts are common among large institutional traders, since this is one
of the ways they can move thousands of contracts without adversely affecting
their profitability. Weekly charts tend to exhibit much less volatility, and the
continuity of thought tends to last longer. Traders incorporating monthly and
weekly data use much larger stops than a similar methodology using a shorter
time frame. Daily charts are where the bulk of the traders live and die. The
level of volatility is naturally higher, and the stops are smaller, in daily charts.
Traders using charts constructed from hourly, *n* minute, and tick charts have
the tightest, smallest stops and also experience the most volatility.

Regardless of your time frame for trading, you can always use a larger or
smaller time frame to analyze the markets. It is critical that after you decide
what time frame you will trade from, you stick to that time frame. It is also
critical that you take every signal that your methodology generates from your
chosen time frame. Naturally there is an exception to this rule, and that is if
the next longer time frame than what you are trading in, indicates a major
possibility of a break in the continuity of thought. Then you might want to
enter into the trade with fewer contracts or decide to pass on the deal. However, you must have predefined what the longer time frame must be doing to
make you pass on what your methodology is telling you to do.

Here is another example. As I write, May corn is creating a sell signal
according to my methodology on a daily chart. However, on the weekly
corn chart my methodology indicates that in all probability the continuity
of bearish thought that has created the present bear market is broken.
Therefore I decide not to take the sell signal that I normally would take.
Now at this point in time I have no idea if corn will continue down or if we
are about to enter a bull market. What I do know is that with everything I
can discern in this instant of time, there is a high probability that the continuity of bearish thought has changed. Whether the bears will build a consensus of opinion and reestablish their continuity of bearish thought
remains to be seen. What I am certain of, though, is that if the bears do in
fact reestablish their continuity of thought, I will get short as quickly as my
methodology allows.

Your entry point strategy and exit point strategy are interwoven with
each other and with the way you perceive the market. There is no one perfect

strategy. Likewise, there is no "incorrect" way to enter the market—provided you have developed, back-tested, refined, and then finally tested your strategy in real time. There most definitely is a wrong way to enter or exit a market. This incorrect way is to use a strategy developed by someone else, one that you have not internalized within you and that you apply inconsistently. There is nothing inherently wrong with using an indicator developed by someone else, provided you have validated the ability of this indicator to perform to *your standards*. You accomplish this by back testing, validating, possibly customizing the indicator, and then finally testing the strategy or indicator in real time.

I sincerely hope that by now you are beginning to understand how placing your faith in a purchased program or get-rich trading book is the certain path to misery and financial ruin. Developing your methodology to determine the continuity of thought, and the strategy to determine where to enter and where to exit, is not easy. If it was easy, everyone would be trading—and driving around in a Ferrari!

18

MONEY MANAGEMENT STRATEGIES

Focus on exiting strategies rather than trade initiating param-eters. The big money is captured by managing risk with exits.

—CHRISTOPHER R. CASTROVIEJO

In my early days, I didn't have the staying power—psycho-logically, emotionally, and, most important, financially.

—JIMMY ROGERS

I formed my own opinion of the stock's value, and after the stock began to back down from its top price, I took a bearish position in it which I later extended.

—BERNARD E. "SELL 'EM BEN" SMITH

MONEY MANAGEMENT OR risk control strategies are the most critical requirement for a successful trader. Without exception, every outstanding trader will tell you that it is *the* most important factor that determines your success. All traders starting out make many mistakes, and are constantly making learning distinctions. As these traders obtain good judgment, they will make many new learning distinctions. Unfortunately, most new learning distinctions result in a loss of equity. Traders who have risk control strategies will be able to survive these errors. Without risk control parameters, the likelihood of losing a large percentage of trading capital will be overwhelming. The preservation of capital is a primary consideration. It is the underlying concept of all money management strategies.

While I was working for Lind-Waldock, one of the differences that was very obvious between novice and professional traders (besides their belief structure) was how the professional trader followed very strict risk control procedures, and the amateur trader had none. Risk management strategies have a huge impact on the amount of profit generated. Other, lesser factors that affect the amount of profit generated include the amount of money in the account, the trading methodology, and the experience of the trader. This is the longest chapter of the book. Without the ability to preserve your capital, you will exhaust your trading capital before you have developed your beliefs or methodology.

IMPORTANCE OF RISK CONTROL

The primary reason risk control strategies are more important than trading methodology is that the trading strategy, regardless of how well it has been researched and back-tested and regardless of its profitability, *could lose money*. Every time a trader enters into a new trade the risk is always guaranteed. Whether that new trade generates a profit or a loss depends on variables unique to that trade. Traders want to manage their equity so it is steadily increasing. The equity curve, if plotted, should show a steadily increasing arc with many small high and low points, much like a saw blade that is slanting upward. It should not show huge up and down equity swings. Should the deviation or the swings be too great, the trader will eventually lose all capital. Figure 18-1 summarizes the curves.

FIGURE 18-1   Good/Bad Equity Curves

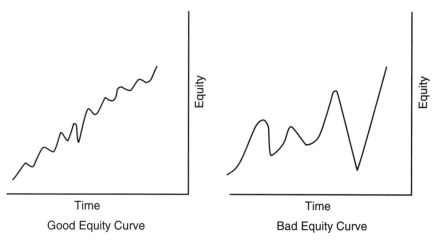

Good Equity Curve   Bad Equity Curve

ESSENCE OF MONEY MANAGEMENT

The essence of money management is how well a trader manages his or her equity. Whenever we think of risk or reward, we must always keep in mind the total potential profit or loss, and the probability of that profit or loss occurring.

Dependent

The trader's equity curve is dependent upon the reward-to-risk ratio. Risk depends on the amount of uncertainty that is inherent in a trade or in the market. The amount of risk is largely dependent upon the time frame under consideration.

Independent

The trader's equity curve is independent of any trading methodology. The trader's methodology should give an indication of the amount of risk and reward in the potential move—for example, a double bottom or a rising wedge formation.

Critical Distinction

The critical distinction is that there is no limit to the upside. Profitability could increase 50 percent or even 500 percent. However, there is a limit to the amount of money the equity could drop. A drop of 100 percent results in all trading stopping.

Risk can be defined as the probability that a trade or a series of trades will result in a loss of equity. Many novice traders define risk very simply as the amount of money they could lose on a particular trade (i.e., where their protective stop is). Occasionally the more astute novice trader will define risk as the entire amount in their trading account.

Profit is the trader's reward for doing the right "things" at the right time.

"Great traders are evaluated."

Traders who either trade other people's money as commodity trading advisers (CTAs) or are employed by corporations or funds are evaluated on the basis of how much profit was made versus how much was lost. The amount of knowledge they possess concerning technical or fundamental analysis is irrelevant in the final judgment. Technical analysis could give an indication of the amount of risk and the possible gain in a potential move— for example, in a double bottom or a head and shoulders formation. Fundamental analysis can also provide an indication of the risk and reward potential. All great traders know that in order to be successful they must truly understand the concept of risk and reward. Professional traders are constantly striving to reduce risk, while trading with discipline.

FACTORS AFFECTING RISK

Time

As shown in Figure 18-2, the amount of risk a trader's equity is subjected to usually increases with the length of time the trade is held, however at a decreasing rate. The amount of risk in placing a trade should always be less for trading in shorter time frames. For example, a trader who is trading off a 5-minute chart should be risking less money per trade than a trader who is trading off a daily chart. Risk and time generally act in lockstep unison. Risk decreases with less time, and increases as time increases.

FIGURE 18-2   Risk and Time

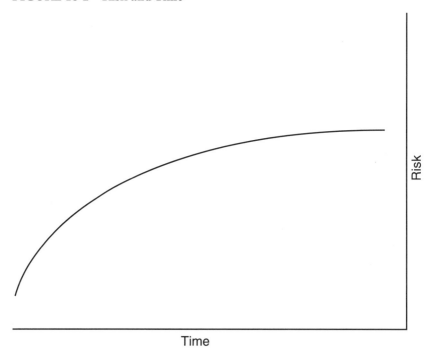

A trader's goal is to be in a trade for the least amount of time, thereby reducing risk, and for long as possible to increase the possible profit. It is critical to understand that risk always increases over time; however, profit potential does not. A profitable trade in a nontrending market is dependent on the timing of the entry and the exit. In a trending market the timing of the entry and exit is of less importance. As a position is held over time the risk is constantly increasing, albeit at an ever-decreasing rate. However, the profit potential is not. Consequently holding a slightly profitable position too long will increase the risk enough to negate any profit potential. Since the market is unpredictable, the longer a trade is held, the higher the probability that there could be an unexpected adverse price movement.

Volatility

Volatility measures how price changes over a certain period of time. The most effective measure of volatility is as a percentage of change. For example, if the price was $100 and it increases to $105, it was a 5 percent change, just as a stock that was at $20 has a 5 percent gain when the price goes to $21. Typically as a market becomes more volatile it becomes more risky, and vice versa. The volatility of a market can change over time. A market can quite easily go from low volatility to high volatility overnight. This is often because of unexpected or important news. Likewise, a market that is highly volatile can suddenly become very quiet again, often because of news. Typically the latter transition (from high to low volatility) takes longer, since markets require more time to calm down than they take to get excited.

An excellent example is the grain market. The grain market can exhibit periods of high volatility primarily because of weather patterns that could affect or are affecting crops. As the volatility of a market increases the risk, the profit potential increases as well. It is important to remember that the *unavoidable and uncontrollable risk* (which we will discuss shortly) will always increase—it is guaranteed. Likewise, the profit *potential* is also guaranteed to increase; *however, profits are not guaranteed.* Many novice traders forget that even though their potential profit increases as the market becomes more volatile, the unavoidable and uncontrollable risks are also constantly increasing. A major problem with a market that is experiencing high volatility is the slippage factor. In addition, the bid/ask spread widens to infinity in a fast-moving market, resulting in horrible fills. Generally a trending market has higher volatility; however, the reverse is not necessarily true. The market can be very volatile with no trend evident. Entering a market that is exhibiting high levels of volatility can be a nerve-wracking experience for many traders.

Consequently many traders think that a market with low volatility is better to trade in. However, low volatility may indicate that there isn't enough price movement for profit. The reward-to-risk ratio may suggest that it is a poor opportunity to trade. Low-volatility markets typically have a lot of random price movements (i.e., the locals in the pit are moving the market) or congested price patterns. In addition, markets with low volatility often have increased costs of trading. Problems with bid/ask spreads, commissions, and lack of price movement tend to reduce the already small profit potential offered by a low-volatility market. As a trader, you must do the research to compare present volatility with historical volatility. The novice trader is best served trading a market that is exhibiting a relative moderate level of volatility.

DIFFERENT TYPES OF RISK

Avoidable Risk

Avoidable risk is risk that can be avoided or reduced without affecting the potential gain. For example, risk of a bad fill can be reduced by using limit orders, avoiding markets with excess volatility, or avoiding markets with very little liquidity. Avoidable risk can also be reduced by proper diversification of the securities traded. We shall shortly see that trading in uncorrelated markets substantially reduces our avoidable risk. Order execution is an area in which many novice traders make mistakes, subjecting their equity to a certain amount of avoidable risk. There are huge differences between a day order, a good till cancel (GTC) order. Limit orders are quite different from market orders. There are procedures that a trader can implement to reduce this risk practically to zero.

Another area (although somewhat mundane) of avoidable risk is anticipating problems that are related to the process of placing orders with the brokerage house. Possible problems include the trading house phone lines going down, the Internet connection failing, and adverse weather affecting the satellite feed. In all these cases, with proper preplanning the trader can reduce and often eliminate these types of risks.

As the volume of trades increases, a trader will occasionally lose money because of an avoidable risk that was not adequately taken care of. Sometimes it can be fairly mundane. I remember trading bonds off a tick chart in 1994, and suddenly my satellite feed crashed. After a quick phone call to a fellow trader to see if he was still getting his data (he was), I looked out the window and realized that because of my intense focus on the price action, I was oblivious to the fact that it was snowing rather intensely. I quickly ran outside to sweep the snow off my satellite dish. The point is that regardless of how much forethought you put into reducing and removing avoidable risk, occasionally an unplanned event will throw you off.

Unavoidable Risk

Certain risks are unavoidable without affecting the overall potential gain of a trade. There are two types of unavoidable risk: controllable and uncontrollable.

Inherent Yet Somewhat Controllable Risk Inherent in every trade is a certain amount of risk. We can attempt to control our loss by predefining what our acceptable loss will be—or what we are willing to risk. Typically we do this by placing a protective stop. In other words, if we're buying 100 shares at $10 each, we can place a stop loss at $9.50, thereby controlling our risk at 50 cents per share. The difficult part of inherent yet controllable risk is that we know how much we want to risk, yet we cannot limit our loss to that amount because of the unavoidable and uncontrollable risk inherent in the trade.

A far more insidious unavoidable risk for most traders is the possibility of a series of unprofitable trades taking place. Typically traders lose more equity from this factor than from any other type of risk. Experiencing a series of losing trades is unavoidable; however, with proper money management strategies the losses can be controlled—even if the string of losses cannot be. The dollars at risk are a function of the trading system's probability distribution, which we will discuss shortly. Consequently this type of risk is difficult to ascertain without some fairly advanced math.

Unavoidable and Uncontrollable Risk Some risks are impossible to determine or control before the trade is placed. They become obvious only after the trade is entered, and in some cases exited. In other words, you can place a stop at $9.50 so that if the stock drops suddenly, your protective stop will be activated; however, your fill could be considerably less (e.g., $9.00). Once you enter into a trade, your equity is subject to unavoidable and totally uncontrollable risks. Here are the most common.

1. Overnight risk. Whenever the market is closed and you are unable to exit your position, you are subjecting your equity to overnight risk. Often the market will open at a different price from where it closed because of bearish or bullish overnight news. If a market opens adversely to your position, the amount of loss you experience will be more than you wanted. In other words, if you are long bonds at $120^{12}/_{32}$, with a protective stop at $119^{31}/_{32}$, and the market opens at $119^{20}/_{32}$, you will be stopped out at a much lower price than you were expecting.

In a desire to eliminate overnight risk, some traders only day-trade exiting all positions before the close. The downside is that these traders eliminate *favorable* gap opens, and increase their transactional costs. (More trading increases the commissions paid and the amount of slippage experienced.) In effect they are substituting overnight risk for sometimes much higher transactional costs. Overnight risk is often followed by liquidity risk when the market opens (increasing the slippage a day trader experiences). A trader can get a good understanding of the overnight risk by researching the frequency of gap openings and amount of that difference. Really large gap opens occur infrequently, and very rarely are more than 5 to 10 percent of the price of the underlying contract.

2. Liquidity risk.   The market sometimes becomes illiquid enough so that you get filled at prices that adversely affect your equity. Often whenever the liquidity of a normally liquid market becomes thin, it means that the market could be at a turning point. Whenever a normally liquid market experiences low liquidity, the price is generally moving quickly in one direction, resulting in price slippage. Typically liquidity risk increases whenever there is crucial news or a government report is released. Whenever liquidity dries up there is a price vacuum, resulting from an imbalance of orders due to the news event or a lot of stop orders at certain price levels.

The more the liquidity of the market dries up, the worse the price slippage becomes. Every market will at times experience liquidity problems; however, some markets experience liquidity problems more often. For example, bonds are very liquid, and typically you can get filled within one tick of where you desire to enter the market. Sugar and coffee are very thin markets, and the liquidity can be quite poor.

Determining liquidity risk is often difficult. This is because a normally liquid market may experience no liquidity problems for a relatively long period of time. Then an unexpected news event catches the market by surprise, and the liquidity disappears. The best way to determine liquidity risk is by looking at tick charts that encompass several days. This allows you to see the amount of price movement tick by tick. If a tick chart indicates that trading is taking place at intervals of one or two ticks, then the market is demonstrating good liquidity. If trades are taking place at tick intervals of three or more, then the liquidity is poor. The critical assumption is that you are looking at "normal" trading days. Another way to determine liquidity is to look at the volume of contracts that are traded in that particular market. Typically the higher the volume, the more liquid the market.

A limit move is an extreme example of a market with no liquidity. Some exchanges place a limit on how much and how far the price may move in one day. A limit move is the result of no one being willing or able to take the opposite side of the trade. Limit move risk is a subset of liquidity risk because the trader, by being on the wrong side of the move, is unable to exit the trade.

REDUCING, MANAGING, AND CONTROLLING RISK

Inherent in every trade is a certain element of risk. All successful traders always know the amount of risk that they are subjecting their portfolio to, and will do everything possible to reduce this risk. They will then enter into their trade with the expectation that the market could do anything and that they have accepted all the risk. The most common way to reduce avoidable or unavoidable risk is by diversifying a portfolio.

Diversification

Diversification enables traders to earn the same or higher profits while experiencing the same or a lesser amount of avoidable risk. Typically traders will diversify their portfolio by either trading contracts that are not highly correlated or trading different methodologies. Why do most traders decrease their portfolio, and increase their cash holdings when they are nervous? Because cash doesn't correlate to anything (the common belief).

In order to properly diversify your portfolio, you must understand the concept of correlation. Correlation occurs when a security (stock, commodity, or derivative) reacts to another security in a positive, negative, or neutral manner. Two securities that are *positively* correlated will rally and decline in price in lockstep with each other. Good examples are T-bills and T-bonds, or the S&P 500 and the DJIA, which normally track each other. A perfectly *negatively* correlated security is inversely in lockstep with another. Instead of both going up together, one of the securities will rally and the other one will drop. Typically a negatively correlated market is the T-bond market and the CRB Index. Since the CRB generally tracks the inflationary forces in the United States, and bonds are adversely affected by inflation, whenever the CRB increases in price, bonds will decline in price. Figure 18-3 shows a negative correlation. Markets that are neutrally correlated move in a random fashion to each other. A good example is orange juice and crude oil.

The interesting thing is that the correlation factor between the different markets can strengthen or disappear overnight. The correlation factor is in a constant state of flux. There are times when the U.S. Treasury bond market could be positively correlated to the Dow Jones Industrial Average, and yet other times when they will be negatively correlated. Different markets can become correlated because of specific news events that affect their fundamental picture; at other times the correlation stops because of the news.

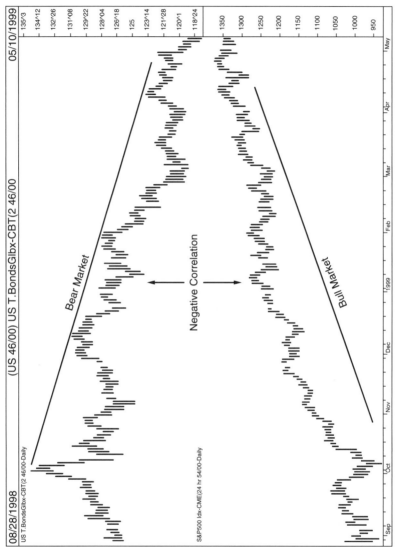

FIGURE 18-3 Negative Correlation

171

Markets can become highly correlated for short periods of time. They become correlated very quickly based upon news that tends to affect the fundamental picture. The more you understand the fundamentals behind each market, the better you'll be able to understand how different markets can become correlated. It is fascinating to consider how markets become correlated, and to consider the implications of what one market is doing and how it might affect another market. For example, whenever I decide to place a trade in live cattle, I also monitor the price action in lean hogs—*provided they are positively correlated.* As soon as I see a price action in either live cattle or lean hogs that indicates it is time to enter into the trade, I do so. In some cases, for example, I want to get long in cattle, and yet the price action that I need to actually pull the trigger may not be present in cattle but will be present in hogs. If I had waited for the price action in cattle, I would have missed the trade. Studying market relationships is a truly fascinating endeavor.

It is important to remember that markets can become highly correlated (positive or negative) or uncorrelated very quickly for very short or very long periods of time. What determines this is the underlying news that causes the commodities to become correlated. The more that traders understand the fundamentals of each market, the more they begin to understand correlation factors. At certain periods of time interest rates/stocks, gold/crude bonds/stocks/crude, exchange rates/interest rates, crude/soybeans have all been either positively or negatively correlated.

Just as there can be a correlation factor between different markets, so there can be a correlation factor between the different methodologies a trader develops. When a trader diversifies on the basis of methodologies, it is crucial to use methodologies that are not correlated to each other.

Market Diversification   Diversifying into different markets is the most common method by which a trader manages risk. As different markets that have little correlation are added to the portfolio, the amount of avoidable risk is reduced. The amount of avoidable and unavoidable risk reduction that is provided by trading three or four uncorrelated markets is very significant. The level of risk reduction continues to be reduced, albeit at a slower rate, until approximately eight uncorrelated contracts are being traded. According to most studies, diversifying into more than eight different markets is only slightly beneficial.

It is important that the markets diversified into have the same, if not better, liquidity. The benefits of increased diversification can easily be lost by using less liquid markets. In addition, as the number of markets that are traded increases, the more time the trader will have to spend studying these markets. As a trader examines the additional markets it could be at the expense of the original market, consequently reducing the overall performance. A proper balance is required to reduce the amount of risk that the equity is subject to. A trader must use contracts that have enough liquidity and are not correlated. The cost of not diversifying enough is a high level of avoidable risk. The cost of too much diversification is reduced performance, caused by excessive unavoidable risk.

However, if the markets traded are highly correlated and cannot be reduced in number for whatever reason, the trader must reduce the number of contracts traded. For example, if you are trading one contract each of the German mark, British pound, Swiss franc, and Australian dollar, then as far as risk control is concerned you could be trading just four contracts in one market instead of one contract in four markets. This is because currencies are usually positively or negatively correlated. In other words, the amount of leverage used in a highly correlated portfolio should be adjusted down when compared with a portfolio consisting of diversified markets.

Trading leverage is more commonly defined as the number of contracts traded in each market, and should be adjusted upward or downward so the amount of equity risked is not more than 3 percent. More on this later.

Time Frame Diversification   Overall risk can be reduced by developing a methodology that examines the price action of the same market while utilizing different time frames and different entry and exit times. In other words, a trader could have one multiple contract entry, and then have multiple exits based upon applying the trading methodology to different time frames. Alternatively a trader could have multiple entries in the same contract, and use one common exit. For example, a trader could go long ten corn contracts, and then exit two contracts based upon the price action of a 5-minute chart. The trader could then exit another two contracts based upon the price action of an hourly chart, eventually exiting the other six contracts based upon the price action of the daily, weekly, and monthly chart. By doing this, the trader is able to catch the very short move and the longer-term move—in other words, to stay with the trend. Likewise, a trader could scale into a large position using multiple time frames.

The only variable is the time frame used; the trader's methodology and the underlying contract remain the same.

Methodology Diversification   A trader utilizing different methodologies is diversifying risk. For example, a methodology that works well in a trending market could underperform in a nontrending market. By allocating some equity with a methodology that performs well in a trending market, and also allocating a percentage with a methodology that performs well in a nontrending market, the trader is reducing risk.

Often one methodology will be long in one market, while a different methodology could be long (or short). These different methodologies and markets tend to reduce the amount of risk being experienced. By adding a methodology that has a lower rate of return than their primary methodology, traders can actually increase the overall return! The assumption here is that the markets being traded are not highly correlated, so that the risk reduction gained by diversification of methodologies is greater than the decline in the overall return and the *leverage factor is adjusted accordingly!*

1. Monitoring the liquidity of a market. Traders can reduce risk by carefully monitoring the liquidity of the markets they are trading in. Generally the higher the volume, and the higher the open interest, the more liquid the market is. Stock traders need be concerned only about volume. There is an interesting relationship between liquidity and volatility. As the volatility of a market increases, so does the inherent and unavoidable risk—with an increase of profit potential. However, as the liquidity of a market increases, the inherent and unavoidable risk decreases—without affecting the profit potential. Liquidity and volatility are two different animals, and should not be confused. Although a lack of liquidity could be caused by high volatility, a lack of volatility is not caused by a lack of liquidity. Likewise, high volatility is not dependent on a lack of liquidity.

The vast majority of commodity traders should examine the volume of trades when ascertaining the level of liquidity, rather than the amount open interest. A market that has a lot of open interest and little volume is typically less liquid than a market with little open interest and lots of volume. In most cases, only the very large traders and commercials hedgers pay a lot of attention to open interest in determining the liquidity of the market. The reason is that they need to know how their trades will affect the market. If the open interest is small, they have to think about who will take the other side of their position upon entering or exiting the trade. The liquidity of a market becomes a self-feeding circle—that is, a market with a lot of liquidity tends to attract even more traders, making it even more liquid.

The more liquid contract in a particular market is the contract you need to be trading. If it is currently June, why trade December when the September contract has more volume or liquidity? In most cases December will not have as much liquidity as September. Determining the more liquid month is as easy as opening the newspaper and reading the number of contracts traded.

Typically the higher the liquidity for the chosen market, the lower the cost of entry (i.e., less slippage). Treasury bonds, for example, have a very negligible cost of execution, whereas platinum can be very expensive. A speculator thrives on liquidity as a way to control risk, and is hurt by avoidable risk.

2. *Monitoring the volatility of a market.*   Whenever the volatility changes, trading leverage should be adjusted accordingly. As the volatility increases the likelihood of an adverse price movement increases; therefore, the number of contracts should be reduced. Likewise, as the volatility diminishes, the possibility of an adverse price movement diminishes and the leverage factor can be adjusted upward. This rule is of great benefit if adhered to. The reason is that whenever the continuity of thought changes, many large emotional mood swings will be reflected in the price. Therefore when the leverage, or number of contracts traded, is reduced, the number of contracts held at a market turn will be reduced as volatility increases. The volatility of a market is related to some degree to liquidity and the bid/ask spread.

The Bid/Ask Spread Risk   The bid/ask spread is an indication of market liquidity. As the spread loosens, the amount of money lost upon entering or exiting the trade will also increase. In other words it is a market commission for entering and exiting a trade. As the liquidity of a market increases, the bid/ask spread becomes tighter. By contrast, an illiquid market will have a wide bid/ask spread. Another way to see the bid/ask spread risk is as an approximate indication of the number of participants. An interesting aspect of a market that is locked limit up or down is that typically the bid/ask spread will narrow in the front and back month. This is because, in a lock limit move, you are still allowed to trade spreads. Typically a trader will execute a spread then break a leg in order to exit a lock limit market.

Reducing the Risk of a Series of Losses   Another practice that many outstanding traders implement when they start having a losing streak is to reduce the number of contracts traded until the losing streak breaks. By reducing their exposure to the market, they are able to prevent a losing streak from becoming a major retracement of their equity. Generally they know that the losing streak has ended when the red ink fades and black ink is consistently appearing.

The important thing to remember is that you should not get into a position where your trading equity is overcommitted, so that a series of bad trades could consume your equity and halt your trading efforts.

Using Stops to Reduce Risk   In order to limit the maximum amount of loss acceptable on a particular trade, the trader will generally place a stop loss order every time a trade is entered. In most cases it will be a GTC (good till cancel) order. This stop loss order will also keep the trader from procrastinating about exiting a losing trade.

Stops are used as a protective measure to help decrease the risk that an account is exposed to. Stops can be used for an entry or exit strategy or for protective risk management. Stops that are used for risk management can be categorized in two ways:

- A *price stop* will get the trader into or out of a trade if a predetermined price is hit.

- A *time stop* will get the trader out of a trade whenever a certain amount of time has elapsed.

Perhaps the most important aspect of trading is the correct placement of protective stops. Before entering a trade, the trader must always predetermine where to exit the trade if the market fails to behave as expected.

It is important to remember that the longer a trade is held, the more risk a trader is exposed to. A protective stop placed too close to the market action will virtually guarantee the trader of being stopped out. If the stop is too far away, it loses its effectiveness. The amount of money that would be lost over time by using a protective stop is in large part determined by the percentage of winning to losing trades. By changing the profit and loss objectives, the trader will change the percentage of winning to losing trades. If the percentage of winning to losing trades is 50 percent, a trader must profit more than the amount placed at risk in order to be profitable. However, if the percentage of winning to losing trades is higher, a trader can earn less than the amount risked and still remain profitable. Likewise, if the percentage of winning to losing trades is less than 50 percent, a trader must make more than the amount risked to be net profitable.

A protective stop can be placed at a price level where the pattern that generated the entry signal has obviously been negated. For example, if the reason for going long was the formation of a double bottom, then placing the stop under the double bottom would be a logical place. The reason it is logical is that, should the price decline so that the stop was triggered, then obviously our perception of a double bottom was incorrect. By placing our stop at a price that indicates our entry reason was incorrect, we have been able to define our risk. If we are stopped out, we are able to preserve our equity and wait for another opportunity to present itself.

The amount of money a trader should risk in a trade is determined by various factors. The important concept to understand is that the stop placement location is independent of the amount of money the trader wants to risk. A protective stop should be placed at important technically derived price points. In general this seems to work best at important price levels that were generally respected in prior market activity. Should the penetrated price that would represent a failure of the pattern used to enter into the market represent a monetary loss that exceeds what you are willing or able to accept, then you must pass on the trade. In other words, if your methodology recognizes a certain market pattern indicating that you should get long, and you determine that the nearest significant price that would represent failure of that pattern exceeds the amount of money that your rules permit, then you must not make the trade.

Another thing to remember is that the market you are looking at will move a certain amount each day. If the amount that you are risking is less than the amount the market typically moves in one day, you are virtually guaranteed to be stopped out—unless you have an instant winner. In other words, if you are trading U.S. Treasury bonds using daily data, and you are willing to risk only $200 in a market that typically moves $1000 every day, then you're almost guaranteed to be stopped out with a loss. If the amount of money that you are able to risk as determined by your risk parameters is only $200, you should find an acceptable market that moves $200 or less in one day.

The market can become very volatile instantly. If your protective stop is on the wrong side of the market when the volatility suddenly increases, you will quite naturally be stopped out. Generally this might not be so bad, since it typically means that the trade was not the right one. Your protective stop should not be your exit strategy, unless your exit methodology is to use a trailing stop.

Protective stops are used to limit the amount of loss experienced by the trader in case there is a huge move against the trade. A stop loss order does not guarantee that you will get filled at that price (your fill could be even more adverse to your position than you would want). It does mean that you will get out (provided the huge move isn't a limit move). It is not meant to replace your exit strategy, as discussed in the previous chapter. The protective stop is intended only to get you out of your position. Placing protective stops can be more of an art than a science. I like to place my stop at a price level that indicates a sudden and decisive change in the continuity of thought. The question I ask is: "At what price area would the force that I am aligned with be in total disarray, beating a hasty retreat?" Once I can determine this price area, I place my protective stop just beyond it. Another factor to keep in mind is that as the volatility increases, the protective stop becomes wider, increasing the possible loss if the stop is elected.

There are two concerns when placing a protective stop. The first is the amount of money at risk. The second is where the stop is placed. Both of these need to coincide; otherwise a protective stop is just a limitation point loss, and not a pivotal point in the market.

Suppose you just went long gold at 301, and there is massive support at 290. You can assume that if the bears suddenly gain strength and start forcing the price down toward 290, the bulls should begin to defend the 290 price area. If the bulls are not strong enough to overcome the selling pressure of the bears, and the price declines to under 290, then the bulls will *probably* begin to panic. By liquidating their long positions, they will add more strength to the bears, driving prices even lower. Therefore you would be safe in placing your stop at 289 or 288. You don't want to be long if the bears hit 288, as it would represent that the bears are the stronger force.

PROFITABILITY

The reason most traders lose their trading equity is poor risk control. Whereas profitability is always desired, it is losses that a trader must be constantly on guard against. The profitability of a trade is never assured; however, the risk is. Trading profits allow us to play one more day; excessive losses prevent us from playing any more. Traders who focus only on profits will often lose all their equity, because of uncontrolled risk taking stemming from their beliefs. However, traders who focus only on risk will never be able to make the trade, because they will prefer to keep their equity in cash.

Determining the Expected Outcome

Calculating the expected outcome of a trade is a simple way to look at risk and reward. When we calculate the expected outcome, we're looking at the combined chances of a profit and a loss. When we use expected outcome, we can get an indication of whether a strategy will be profitable in the foreseeable future. In most cases a severe loss due to uncontrolled risk factors is rarely more than 10 percent of the contract price.

Professional traders will always consider the risk involved in a potential trade versus the potential profit. Novice traders typically focus only on the amount of profit in a potential trade; consequently they lose a lot of their money. An experienced trader uses a mathematical formula to examine how risk and profit relate and to calculate the expected outcome of a trade. This is important because a trader must focus on the combined picture of profit and loss. By thinking about how a particular trade might work out, the trader is increasing the probability of ultimate success. The mathematical formula for the expected outcome of any particular trade is simply the sum of the chances of each element of that trade occurring. The formula is:

$$\text{Expected Outcome} = \sum_{i=1}^{n} ab$$

where a = chance of trade event occurring
        b = trade event
        n = total number of trades
        i = period when event occurred

While it looks like a complicated formula, it really is not. In order to determine what the expected outcome of two trades will be, the trader must determine the percentage of winning to losing trades, the amount of average profits, and the average loss. For example, a trader who makes $100 on average for every winning trade and loses $50 on average on every losing trade is 50 percent profitable (hence 50 percent of the time the trader loses). Then we can plug the numbers into the formula and determine the expected profits after two trades.

$$\text{Expected Outcome} = (100 \times .5) + (100 \times .5) - (50 \times .5) - (50 \times .5)$$
$$= \$50$$

Using another example, if a trader makes $75 on average for every winning trade, loses $50 on every losing trade, and is profitable 60 percent of the time (loses 40 percent of the time), then the expected profit after two trades is:

$$\text{Expected Outcome} = (75 \times .6) + (75 \times .6) - (50 \times .4) - (50 \times .4)$$
$$= \$50$$

One last example. A trader makes $100 on winning trades, loses $50 on losing trades, and loses 60 percent of the time (winning 40 percent). The expected profit after two trades is:

$$\text{Expected Outcome} = (100 \times .4) + (100 \times .4) - (50 \times .6) - (50 \times .6)$$
$$= \$20$$

Many mathematical calculators have a summation function that will enable you to easily calculate the outcome after any number of trades. By sitting down one evening and playing with this formula, you will begin to understand how important it is to control your risk exposure, and how important it is to have an effective exit strategy that enables you to keep your profits.

By using this formula, you'll be able to obtain an indication of whether your methodology will be profitable in the future. Every successful trader has developed a methodology that yields a positive number. Unfortunately, most beginning traders have a negative expected outcome with their methodology. Using the expected outcome formula will help you look at the different possibilities and determine if your methodology is financially sound.

Return on Investment (ROI)

Professional traders measure their profitability through a fairly common mathematical formula: return on investment (ROI). The ROI tells us how effectively our capital was used over a period of 12 months. This is the most effective way to determine the performance of our methodology. Whereas beginning traders will measure success on how many winning trades they generate and the dollar amount generated, professional traders will use return on investment as a way to measure the profitability of his methodology. A trader can have 20 profitable trades in a row and return all the profits on the next trade.

$$\text{Return on Investment} = \frac{\text{Net Profit}}{\text{Equity Used}}$$

For example, if a trader has a portfolio at the beginning of the year of $20,000, and by the end of the year has generated a profit of $8000, the rate of return is:

$$\text{ROI} = \frac{8,000}{20,000}$$

$$= 40\%$$

Drawdown of Equity

All traders experience a losing streak. The amount of money the trader loses over time from the previous equity high point is known as a drawdown. A drawdown represents the amount of money lost that must be replaced to return the equity back to the level it was at prior to the initial loss. When

FIGURE 18-4   Maximum Drawdown

	Beginning Equity	Profit	Loss	Ending Equity
January	$20,000.00	$1204.56		$21,204.56
February	21,204.56	485.00		21,689.56
March	21,689.56	8643.25		30,332.81
April	30,332.81		($1804.59)	28,528.22
May	28,528.22		(2043.23)	26,484.99
June	26,484.99	2451.81		28,936.80
July	28,936.80	539.07		29,475.87
August	29,475.87	968.23		30,444.10
September	30,444.10	392.45		30,836.55
October	30,836.55	890.33		31,726.88
November	31,726.88	145.11		31,871.99
December	31,871.99	309.78		32,181.77

traders measure drawdown, they can determine the amount of cash flowing through their account. Maximum drawdown is perhaps the best indication of the amount of risk inherent in a trader's methodology. It is an extremely important concept for all traders. Unfortunately most novice traders, while acknowledging the importance of maximum drawdown, utterly fail to comprehend its true importance. Figure 18-4 illustrates the concept.

To determine your drawdown choose a period of time to examine—typically monthly but sometimes daily. In Figure 18-4 we will look at a monthly summary of all trades over a year. Then begin looking for the first losing trade. Once you have located it, determine equity prior to the loss. In Figure 18-4 the first losing month is April and the equity prior to loss was $30,332.81. Then proceed to the next month, and add the profit or loss to the initial loss. Continue onward until the equity is more or equal to where it was prior to the beginning of the losing month. The largest amount of money that was lost is the drawdown for that period—in this instance $3847.82. Repeat the process with the next losing trade. Once again you will be adding all subsequent gains and losses until all the equity is again recovered.

Maximum drawdown is the largest drawdown you experienced over the entire series of drawdowns that you examined. In Figure 18-4 the largest drawdown was $3847.82. The interesting thing about maximum drawdown is that the longer a trader trades, the more valid the drawdown estimate becomes. Unless there are considerable trades and a considerable number of time periods under consideration, then increasing maximum drawdown by a factor of two, three, or more times more realistically portrays a possible future maximum drawdown. In Figure 18-4 the period of time is only 12 months, consequently we should multiply $3842.82 by at least a factor of .2.

Professional traders always want to know: "What is the worst-case scenario?" The maximum amount of money lost is the maximum drawdown. It indicates the minimum amount of capital we would need without liquidity problems. It serves as an indication of what we could lose in a series of losing trades. It also tells us how often a large loss or a series of losing trades may adversely affect our equity. Maximum drawdown is perhaps the best way to determine risk, since risk is defined as the possibility a particular trade or a series of trades could result in a loss of equity. In order to determine the amount of capital required to trade a particular methodology, margin requirements must be added to the maximum drawdown.

Real-time drawdown attempts to determine how much equity is required to trade a particular methodology. Real-time drawdown is calculated on a day-to-day basis, based on the daily settlement price. While it takes time and effort to determine drawdown in real time, it is the best way to measure the possible future capital requirements.

Always remember that a drawdown of 100 percent means the trader is out of the game. In fact, a drawdown of 50 percent usually means the game is over. Maximum drawdown is a very clear way to determine how well your equity is protected from risk. By determining the maximum drawdown that a trading methodology creates, we can begin to obtain an approximation of the amount of risk our trading capital might be exposed to. The actual drawdown experienced can vary dramatically from theoretical results.

Reward-to-Risk Ratio

The best way to determine profitability of a particular methodology is using the return on investment (ROI) formula to indicate profitability, and measuring risk by using maximum drawdown. When we combine net profit with maximum drawdown as a ratio, we can obtain perhaps the most important ratio in trading: the reward-to-risk ratio. This ratio tells us how much our reward varies with risk. The reward-to-risk ratio will help us to begin to answer several fundamental questions. How much equity is required? And is this a good trading methodology?

The reward-to-risk ratio is very straightforward to calculate. Profits over a period of time divided by the maximum drawdown over the same period of time yields the ratio.

$$\text{Reward-to-Risk Ratio} = \frac{\text{Net Profit}}{\text{Maximum Drawdown}}$$

For example, if a trading methodology over a certain period of time generates a net profit of $5000, and the maximum drawdown is $1500, then the reward-to-risk ratio is:

$$\text{Reward-to-Risk Ratio} = \frac{5000}{1500} = 3.333 \text{ to } 1$$

To obtain a percentage, multiply the number by 100.

$$3.333 \times 100 = 333\%$$

In other words, a trader would be risking $1 to obtain $3.33. However, maximum drawdown does not encompass the total risk that a trader's equity is subjected to. This is because of unavoidable and uncontrollable risk factors. Consequently many professional traders multiply the maximum drawdown by a multiple amount to obtain a more realistic indication of the amount of money that could be required trading a particular methodology. So for purposes of illustration we could multiply the maximum drawdown of $1500 by 2. This gives us the following:

$$\text{Reward-to-Risk Ratio} = \frac{5000}{1500 \times 2}$$

$$= 1.667 \text{ to } 1$$

$$= 166\%$$

As you can see, this changes the overall perception of the profitability of a particular methodology. In Figure 18-4 our reward-to-risk ratio is 1.58 to 1 (using a drawdown factor of 2).

Here is another example, using two different trading methodologies. The first methodology has an equity curve that steadily increases with small gains and small drawdowns. The second methodology has large gains as well as large drawdowns. However, at the end of 12 months both methodologies have a profit of $6000. The first methodology has a maximum drawdown of $1000; the second methodology has a maximum drawdown of $3000. By using drawdowns as an indication of risk, we can see that the second methodology is three times more risky than the first. If we take into account uncontrollable risk factors, and multiply the drawdown of both methodologies by 2, we can obtain a more clear understanding of the actual reward-to-risk ratio.

Methodology 1

$$\text{Reward-to-Risk Ratio} = \frac{6000}{1000 \times 2}$$

$$= 3:1$$

Methodology 2

$$\text{Reward-to-Risk Ratio} = \frac{6000}{3000 \times 2}$$

$$= 1{:}1$$

When we examine the reward-to-risk ratio, we can see that the second methodology besides being three times more risky in terms of drawdowns, also has a terrible reward-to-risk ratio. It makes little sense to risk $1 when the potential gain is limited to $1. The first methodology is risking $1 to have the potential gain of $3.

The vast majority of novice traders fail to adequately look at reward-to-risk ratios. A lot of successful traders are profitable, yet they lose on 60 percent of their trades, winning only 40 percent of the time. The question then arises: If the majority of the times they make a trade they lose, how are they profitable? The answer logically is that when they do win, they win enough to make up for their losses by a healthy percentage. Consequently excellent traders strive to create a methodology that can generate a profit objective, commensurate with where their protective stop would have to be.

In addition, as traders look at various markets and perceive different profit opportunities, they can rank the viability of the various trades by their reward-to-risk ratio. In order to pay for their losing trades, traders must look for the trades whose profit potential exceeds the probability of losses. They do so by ascertaining the profit potential in a particular trade, and the correlated risk. The most commonly used ratio among professional traders is a reward-to-risk ratio of 3 to 1. In other words, while monitoring the various trading opportunities the market is presenting to them, these traders look for a trade that will allow them to risk losing $1 with the probability that they will earn $3. This strategy then allows them to use their capital most effectively.

A reward-to-risk ratio should be based on probability, and successful traders are confident that the probabilities will always come back in their favor. In other words, if a system or methodology demonstrates that the probability of success is greater than 50 percent—say, 65 percent—then 6.5 times out of 10 the trader will win, meaning that losses will occur only 3.5 times out of 10. The art of structuring risk is to recognize that sooner or later the probabilities will come back home; you'll lose those 3.5 times out of 10, and will need to have that amount of drawdown as your risk capital. This is especially true if that 3.5 times out of 10 comes one after the other!

A critical distinction needs to be made here. That distinction is how important volume (or the number of trades a trader makes) is to synthetically create those odds. For example, flipping a coin 10 times may not yield a 50-50 split, but flipping it 1000 times will. Therefore traders need to have enough staying power to "flip" their trading methodology enough times to allow the probabilities to come back into their favor. They must also be involved in trades that are "big" enough, profitwise, so that the 3.5 times they lose, they are able to recapitalize their account. The probability that a trader will experience more consecutive winning/losing trades as the frequency of trading increases is covered in more detail in the next section on probabilities.

That is what the traders' adage "Let profits run and cut losses short" means. The largest profits are achieved only by staying with a winning trade as long as the continuity of thought persists, and your methodology is still indicating that the trade is valid. Generally only a small handful of trades will generate these large profits; it is absolutely essential that these winners be allowed to play out. That is why it is also essential that losses be cut short when they are still small, and before they turn into monster losses.

An interesting thought is that a trader who loses on a great majority of trades, and follows conservative money management rules, will earn more money over a course of several years than a trader who consistently wins on the great majority of trades, and fails to have effective money management rules.

PROBABILITY THEORY

Most traders seldom stop to consider the challenges that are encountered when a series of winning or losing trades occurs. Many traders when considering the likelihood of a string of losing trades will think of Murphy's Law: "Anything that can go wrong will go wrong." Often it does seem that losing begets more losing. Ask mathematicians how you can be more objective, and how you can more clearly define or anticipate the probability of a series of consecutive losing or winning trades, and they will respond with a mathematical formula.

The first thing that we need to know is the probability of a particular event occurring. For example, we know that by flipping a coin the possibilities are that we will get either heads or tails. In other words, the possibility is 50 percent on one coin flip. In order to determine the probability that we will flip the coin two times and have it come up heads both times, we need to use a formula.

The probability of a series of independent events occurring equals the product multiplied by the probability of each event taking place. For example, when a coin is flipped, it has a 50 percent chance of coming up heads. In order to determine the number of times heads can come up four times in a row, all we have to do is multiply 50 percent four times.

$$.50 \times .50 \times .50 \times .50 = .0625$$

The answer is that we have a 6.25 percent probability of heads coming up four times in a row. If we convert 6.25 percent to a fraction, $^1/_{16}$, we can obtain the ratio. In this instance we would have a 1-in-16 chance of getting heads four times in a row. Now let me ask you a question: What is the possibility of heads coming up the fifth time when we flip the coin? The answer is 50 percent; the reason is that each act of flipping the coin is an independent event! However, the probability of five consecutive heads is calculated by multiplying 50 percent by itself five times to arrive at 3.125 percent. Remember, independent events are those events not affected by a prior event. How many traders after experiencing four consecutive winners are not ready to bet everything on the next trade?

This is very interesting and applicable to trading. Many novice traders who have four consecutive winning trades experience euphoria that knows no bounds. Very rarely will novice traders stop to consider the implications of probability theory regarding a series of winning or losing trades. Although a series of winning trades is always great, and beneficial to a trading account, it is the series of losing trades that has the potential to bankrupt the trader. In addition, a series of losing trades is extremely damaging to the trader's emotional, and psychological well-being—enough so that many traders after experiencing a series of losing trades no longer have the desire or the ability to make effective trades.

When considering the possibility of how many losing trades a trader may experience, it is helpful to keep in mind that as the number of trades increases, so does the statistical probability of more frequent and longer sequences of either consecutive winners or consecutive losers. For example, numerous flips of the coin will contain many sequences of consecutive heads, and again many sequences of tails. Naturally, the probability of a particular sequence occurring decreases as its independent repetitions increase. Recall, the probability dropped from 6.25 percent for a series of four heads to 3.125 percent for a series of five heads.

In general when devising a risk strategy, it is best to assume that the probability exists to experience consecutive losing trades. Remember that the probability of experiencing a series of winning/losing trades depends on the trades being totally independent of the prior trade. However, many traders are trading markets and methodologies that are correlated either positively or negatively. Consequently these trades are not independent because they are correlated to each other. This is why the probability of experiencing consecutive losing or winning trades increases while trading. Unlike the independent coin flip, which statistically is 50 percent likely to come up heads or tails, trading is typically *not* an independent affair having 50 percent outcomes. This is because of the trader's methodology, and how he or she perceives the market. As successful traders assert their discipline and trade according to their methodology, they will generate a statistically large enough universe of trades to determine their drawdown and win/loss ratio. For example, if you execute 200 trades using the exact same methodology, by examining your data you could ascertain what percentage of your trades were winning trades. You could then determine the probability of a series of *n* trades being consecutive winners or losers. If you experienced winners, say, 60 percent of the time, you would have a 7.78 percent probability of experiencing five consecutive winning trades, versus 3.13 percent for five coin flips coming up consecutive winners.

As traders gain experience using a particular methodology, the amount they can risk will vary, because now they can begin to ascertain the amount they can risk on the basis of the probability of experiencing consecutive winners or losers. Conversely, beginning traders might think that they have a 50 percent probability of picking a winning trade. This is an illusion, because they are looking at the market with a methodology that they have no experience, confidence or, certainty in. In addition, after a series of losing trades their emotional makeup deteriorates so that they are more likely to choose a losing trade.

EQUITY TO BE RISKED—EQUITY ALLOCATION

All traders are looking for a trading methodology that will rapidly and safely increase their equity curve. After all, it is the equity curve that every trader cares about. The challenge is that if the equity curve increases too slowly (even if it is a safe, smoothly increasing curve), traders become frustrated with how long it's taking to accomplish their goal. Yet if the equity curve increases too rapidly, the drawdowns will probably exceed their capital base, or make them very nervous traders. In other words, the faster the trader's equity increases, the more likely that drawdowns will be severe, and the slower the equity curve increases, the more probable that drawdowns will be moderate.

The goal of every trader is to increase the equity curve somewhere between these two extremes, and to do so as quickly as possible. As you might imagine, this is rarely an easy thing to accomplish. As the equity curve becomes steeper, the amount of risk that the trader's equity is subject to increases, and the faster that equity will increase. As the equity curve becomes less steep, the less the trader's equity is subject to risk, and the slower that equity will increase.

It is a mathematical fact that a 20 percent loss cannot be made back with a 20 percent gain. For example, if you have $100,000 in your trading account and you lose 20 percent, your equity will now be $80,000. If your gain in your next trade is 20 percent, your profit will be $16,000, giving you $96,000. In order to return to your initial equity amount of $100,000, you need to have a gain of 25 percent.

The mathematical formula to determine the percentage required to recover from a loss is:

$$\text{Percent Gain Required} = \frac{\%\ \text{Loss Incurred}}{1 - \%\ \text{Loss Incurred}} \times 100$$

Figure 18-5 depicts the various outcomes graphically. For example, if you lose 50 percent of your equity, you will need to have a 100 percent gain.

$$\text{Percent Gain Required} = \frac{.50}{1 - .50} \times 100$$

$$= \frac{.50}{.50} \times 100$$

$$= 100\%$$

It becomes painfully obvious that a loss of 50 percent makes it almost impossible to recover, since it would take a profit of 100 percent to return to the beginning point. Lost money is always difficult to recoup, because margin requirements and risk management make it ever more difficult to recover from a large drawdown. Every trader has to realize that it is much easier to lose a certain percentage of equity than it is to make it back up and get back to the starting point. This is why risk control and money management are critically important.

Although it sounds impossible, always remember this simple truth: Proper risk management techniques will dramatically increase profits of a marginally good trading methodology; alternatively, an outstanding methodology will lose money if no risk management is practiced.

FIGURE 18-5   Percentage Gain to Recover Percentage Loss

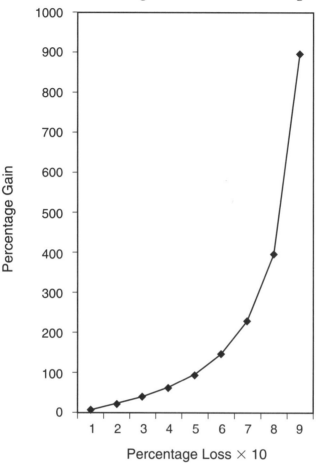

How Much to Risk   The amount of equity to risk will be somewhat dependent upon how risk-averse you are as a trader. It will depend upon the amount of risk that the particular trade or a series of trades is subject to. The amount of equity that can be used on the position size is dependent upon the available equity that can be placed at risk, and is independent of whether a profit or loss has been made. Because of uncontrollable risk, the amount of equity that could be lost is as high as 10 percent; however, it is generally less than 5 percent of the value of the contract. In other words, if you are trading a corn contract that represents 5000 bushels, and corn is currently priced at $2 a bushel, the total value of the corn contract is $10,000. Because of uncontrollable risk factors, the amount of money you could lose would be generally less than $500 (5 percent), and only in extreme cases $1000 (10 percent).

If the combined risk (avoidable and unavoidable) is 10 percent or more, the trader is at extreme risk of losing all equity. This is because ten consecutive losing trades will eliminate all the trader's capital. Contrary to what many beginning traders think, there is a fairly good chance of this taking place. Very rarely are subsequent trades a totally independent event. In addition, markets that were seemingly uncorrelated could become positively or negatively correlated overnight and move against the trader. Consequently subjecting one's equity to a 10 percent risk of loss on a single trade is a very risky proposition. Likewise, risking only 5 percent of equity while removing the probability of losing all the equity by encountering 10 consecutive losing trades does not eliminate the possibility that 50 percent of equity could be lost. As previously mentioned, a 50 percent equity loss demands a 100 percent gain, making it quite likely that the trader will never recover. *This is why most professional traders will risk only 1 to 4 percent of available equity on any one trade.* It is my sincere recommendation that novice traders risk only .5 to 2 percent of equity on any one trade. The percentage of equity that is placed at risk is always based upon the currently available capital.

Risking less equity means that the equity growth will continue to increase, albeit at a slower rate. Risking more equity will increase equity growth at a faster rate — or result in the total loss of equity! Remember that the average successful trader has a profit-to-loss ratio of 1.5 to 2.0, and 25 to 50 percent are profitable trades.

Your equity will increase or decrease on a day-to-day basis. It is of little comfort to be correct in your long-term view — if all your money was lost in the short term. Consequently risking only a small percentage of equity on any one trade will protect your capital. For the most part, professional traders never risk more than 1 to 4 percent of available equity on any one trade. This is because of the ever-present possibility of that particular trade becoming a severe loss owing to uncontrollable risk factors, or a series of losing trades starting with that trade. Trading demands the trader work with and understand probabilities. Consequently professional traders will always understand the probable outcome of any trade. The possible reward must exceed the definite risk exposure of that trade. Professional traders enter into a trade only when the reward-to-risk ratio is in their favor. Professional traders fully understand that they are at the beginning of their equity curve at the start of each trading day. This is an important concept for all beginning traders to comprehend.

While the trading methodology is important, it is the application of valid risk management principles that primarily determine the trader's success or failure.

Margin   Many new traders think that margin is somehow related to risk management. Margin requirements are related only to the amount that the market may move in one day. A margin-to-equity ratio of more than 1 to 5 is excessive, probably resulting in bankruptcy for that particular trader. Overtrading on equity is common among novice traders. Commodity trading involves immense leverage—and the leverage can work both ways. Always remember that risk is a possibility of a loss of equity while in the pursuit of profit.

Common Practices

The majority of professional traders use no more than 50 percent of their total capital to trade with. The other 50 percent is placed in T-bills, earning a little bit of interest. This provides a cushion, or reserve, during drawdowns and losing streaks. In other words, if the total amount of funds deposited with a clearing firm is $100,000, then $50,000 is used to trade with and $50,000 is placed into Treasury bills.

Professional traders monitor the amount at risk as determined by where their exit strategy and stop placement are. Generally no more than 4 percent, and typically 1 to 3 percent, of the total equity is placed at risk on any one trade. So, for example, if there is only $100,000 in the trading account, the trader will place at risk no more than $1000 to $4000. In other words, the trader is willing to lose (risk) no more than 1 to 4 percent on any one particular trade. This naturally limits the number and type of contracts traded, and is accordingly an important consideration.

The trader will also limit the amount of margin deposited for any one market to no more than 25 percent of the total equity. Of the capital that is available to be used for trading, 10 percent will generally be available for margin deposit for any one diversified market. In actuality the amount of total margin in any one market group will vary from 10 to 25 percent. Professional traders will diversify the markets that they trade. This is in order to prevent financial ruin by placing all their trades into one correlated market group. They will also diversify by using different methodologies that they have developed.

Allocation by Diversification   For example, if you are trading Treasury bonds and Swiss francs with $100,000 in your account, then staying within proper risk control parameters, you should normally risk no more than $3000 (3 percent of equity). If the methodology that you are using has average drawdowns of $2000, then you will be limited to trading only one contract in either bonds or Swiss francs. However, if the bonds and Swiss francs are currently trading in an unrelated manner—that is, they are not positively or negatively correlated to each other—then you can trade one contract in each. The only way you could be risking 4 percent ($4000) is if both markets simultaneously lost $2000 on the same day, which is unlikely, since the markets are not currently correlated. The more uncorrelated the markets are, the better the diversification.

Allocation by Number of Contracts   In order to determine the number of contracts to trade, you must determine the maximum drawdown using your trading methodology. Remember that the number of contracts you should trade must be determined by the amount of risk incurred on that particular trade. All too often novice traders will determine the number of contracts they want to trade on the basis of their profit objective or available equity. This is a great way to experience a total loss of equity.

Most novice traders fail to determine what the actual risk may be. This is because the market at any time may do something that is totally unexpected and unanticipated. The trader is usually best advised to consider what the absolute worst-case scenario is, and trade by risking too little rather than risking too much. *Preservation of capital should be of utmost concern to all traders.*

Determining the number of contracts to place within any one particular trade is often difficult. It is so important because it is a key factor in decreasing or increasing the trader's equity curve. Traders must increase the number of contracts traded in order to properly utilize their equity. However, if the number of contracts traded is increased at the wrong time, it will lead to a severe drawdown. Some traders (usually novices) think it's best to increase position size after a series of losses. This is because they believe that a winning run/streak is about to materialize. There are times that the strategy will work, with the winning streak materializing, and the previous drawdown being quickly eliminated. However, it is just as likely that your drawdown could accelerate with the next trade. Consequently increasing position size after drawdowns is generally a poor idea.

Invariably other traders will think that the best strategy for increasing position size is after a series of wins. It doesn't take much genius to realize the tremendous profit potential of increasing position size while experiencing a winning streak. With further contemplation it also becomes obvious that increasing position size because of experiencing a winning streak could result in the trade experiencing a loss or breaking even—if the additional contracts are added at the wrong time. Other traders will increase position size after a series of winning trades, and risk only the amount of previously generated profits.

Typically when traders increase their position size after a series of winning trades, they experience only a large number of breakeven trades. Unfortunately, traders who experience consistent trades that only break even eventually lose all their money. This is because profits must pay for losses. If the vast majority of trades break even, then there are no profits to pay for the losses.

Professional traders have realized that position size is totally dependent upon only one factor. This factor is the amount of capital available to be risked. They have learned from experience that the number of contracts traded is totally independent of whether they are experiencing a profit or a loss. As previously mentioned, poor money management strategies and a great trading methodology will always generate long-term losses. An average trading methodology with proper money management will always generate long-term profits.

A Counterview of Risk Management

Another interesting thing to keep in mind is that the money management rules mentioned so far are based originally on gambling and gaming theories. Unfortunately, a lot of people equate trading with gambling. Naturally if you do not have mastery of your virtues and vices, if you have not done the research and testing to develop your trading methodology and entry/exit strategies, then you are in fact gambling!

When you limit your risk to 5 percent of your total equity, you are in effect giving yourself an opportunity to continue trading up to 19 losers in a row! The problem is that if you have much more than 15 consecutive losses, your remaining capital may not be enough to cover the required margin. Another concept to remember is that the margin you are required to post by the brokerage firm is a *deposit,* and thus is not at risk per se. In actuality your entire net worth is at risk every time you make a trade, even if it is a one-lot yen contract. Don't believe me? Let us say that you opened an account for $5000 and went long on December yen (which happened to be the front contract), requiring a margin deposit of $2500, and your protective stop was $250 lower (5 percent of trading capital). Now, for argument sake, the Russians announce that the Sprately Islands and all the oil in the Sea of Japan is theirs—the Japanese and the Chinese notwithstanding! What do you think the yen will do? That's right, collapse. After four days of downward panic moves (there are no limit moves in the front month) is your loss limited to the $5000 you put up? Hardly. Your house is being auctioned off! So what was your risk? Granted this is an extreme example. However, the underlying concept is totally valid.

Your risk in actuality is your entire net worth. Kind of scary isn't it? "Just great," you must be thinking. "How do I define risk?" The best answer I can give you is that *your risk is the amount that the potential move could adversely affect your equity.* To determine the amount of actual dollars at risk, look at a chart of the contract you are thinking of trading in, and find the last time it had a moderate move up or down (lasting at least a few days). Then calculate how much that move represents in actual dollars. Now multiply that amount by the number of contracts you are intending on trading. It is a real eye-opening exercise, let me tell you. Another concept to remember is that if you go long and a cataclysmic event occurs that makes it impossible to exit the long position, the absolute lowest the contract could fall is to zero. Your maximum loss is defined and limited to the value of the contract. However, going short leaves no finite, defined limit to the potential for a cataclysmic loss, since the value of the contract could theoretically go to the moon.

For example, on 12/30/98 May 1999 corn had a low of 220.5 and rallied for six trading days, and on 1/8/99 it had a high price of 231.0 for a total move of 10.50 cents, or $525. So if you go short on say, 2/10/99, and place a stop at 228.0 risking a couple of cents or $100, in actuality you are risking more like $525. The good news about looking at risk from this perspective is that for all intents and purposes the $525 is the maximum theoretical loss.

SUMMARY

So what is a trader to do? You should realize that as a trader you will be trading your absolutely worst when you first start out. Therefore, you should define exactly what money management rules you are going to employ. For starters I would highly urge you to use the common guidelines of 50 percent of capital for margin deposits, no more than 25 percent of available capital for margin in related markets (preferably less), and no more than 4 percent of total capital on any one trade.

You must be able to define your stop loss point exactly. You must be able to determine what the potential for profit is, and how that relates to the amount of financial risk required to enter into the trade. When you determine your stop loss point and the potential for profit, your rules must be consistent. Your goal is to be able to quantify your strategy and adjust it accordingly. This is possible only when you can define how much you will risk to earn the possible potential profit. Your potential for profit will also require you to have a clearly defined exit strategy.

An analogy sums it up best. If you view the trading environment as a never-ending battle, and your trade as a soldier entering the battlefield, then your "soldier" needs to be conscious of where to run for cover. Similarly where you put your stop is where your trader soldier runs for cover. In other words, prior to putting on a trade, you need to consider a number of things concerning risk profile. These are:

1. Contract liquidity.
2. The possible correlations in your portfolio and the impact of a particular trade on your portfolio risk.
3. The amount of risk inherent in the trade—how far away is the sandbag?
4. The amount of money you want to put into action.
5. Whether the trade is repeatable and can contribute to your methodology probability. (In other words, are you no longer flipping coins, but working with probabilities?) Remember, if a trade isn't repeatable, it probably isn't "retradable" and therefore requires a total dollar risk assessment. If you want to trade the end of the world, make sure it counts. Make sure that if the world doesn't end you still have money and recognize the trade for what it is—a one-time solitary event never likely to repeat, meaning that your probabilities don't exist, which bring in the final criterion.
6. Do you feel lucky?

Every outstanding trader has very strict rules on how to manage risk. Without a very clear strategy, your ultimate success is greatly diminished; with it, your success is almost assured!

19

DEVELOPING A WRITTEN STRATEGY FOR TRADING YOUR METHODOLOGY

What is it that turns ordinary betting into a reckless gamble? Desperation on the part of a heavy loser is one factor.

—BERNARD BARUCH

The simple truth is that there are no "sure things" in the market.

—BERNARD BARUCH

O NE OF THE amazing things about novice traders is that they have not taken the time to write a statement on how they perceive or how they will trade the markets! They might be able to tell you. However, they have not given thought to writing it down. Unfortunately for them, there is a huge difference between being able to tell someone why you did something and writing the reasons down beforehand.

Here is another amazing thing. All the successful traders I have ever met or talked with have written down (in one manner or another) how they see the markets and their exact trading methodology. The rules they live and die by are written down!

I can hear some of you saying, "Yeah, I would too if I could figure everything out." A variation on that sentiment is, "If I had the resources these other traders have, I could write down everything." As you should know by now, you will never figure everything out, and you can never have enough resources. These are excuses that are limiting your profitability. They are limiting beliefs.

Since most traders lose all their trading capital within a fairly short period of time, and since most traders start trading before they have ever written down their views and methodology, doesn't it behoove you to do what all the "other" traders are *not* doing? If you are currently trading, and you do not have a written plan on how you will play the game of trading, then *stop trading*. Do not start trading until you have taken the time to clearly spell out how you perceive the market, what must happen for you to enter, where you will place your stop, what has to happen for you to exit, and most important what your risk management rules are.

Why is this so important? Simple, when you take the time to sit down and write out how you see the market, you are accepting the possibility that you might be wrong. You are beginning to accept responsibility. Once you write down how you perceive the market, the only conclusion you can arrive at, if the market does not behave according to what you wrote, is that your perception was wrong. By writing down that you will enter the market only if certain events transpire, then you are eliminating any possibility that you can blame the market. You are forcing yourself to have consistent discipline.

In other words, if you have taken the time to determine that if the price of a given commodity creates a certain bullish pattern, and your technical indicators do certain bullish things, then you will go long. Should these events occur, and you do not go long, it is obvious that your virtues need to be strengthened. Perhaps the most critical virtues are discipline and integrity. If the trade performs as your research indicated it would, and you were not in the trade, then you can only blame yourself. Likewise, if you consistently enter the trade (upholding your virtues), and you consistently lose, then you will need to determine if your beliefs for getting long are valid. Again this demands adherence to your virtues. It takes a person of strong virtues, with empowering beliefs, to accept that a laboriously devised methodology doesn't perform as expected.

You could have the best rules in the world for getting long, yet the market is starting to turn down and your methodology has not picked up on that fact yet, creating a loss. Consequently there is a fine line between knowing that your methodology is valid, that the market itself is beginning to change, and knowing that your methodology needs to be changed. The more trades that are executed using your methodology, the better you can determine its validity. Just as the RSI needs at least 100 "events" to become valid, so too does your methodology.

When you take the time to write down your rules, beliefs, methodology, and risk management rules about the market, you are transforming your mental reality to a physical reality. No longer will you be able to fudge the numbers, or avoid accepting responsibility. No longer will you be able to "cheat" at trading. All beginning traders want to start trading as soon as they realize the tremendous sums of money that they could have realized if only they had been in the big move that just happened. Hindsight is always 20/20. Novice traders do not have *their own rules.* Consequently they will start trading on the basis of something they read, heard, or learned in a training book or seminar. The rules they are using are the rules that another trader might use successfully. However, they have not taken the time to validate and internalize the references of the other trader. Consequently they will not have the required beliefs to create consistent profits.

By writing down your beliefs about trading, you are forcing yourself to create a series of decisions about the market. You are deciding and committing yourself to how you will perceive the market. By deciding how you will see the market, you are establishing a baseline reference that will prevent you from entering into trades that fail to meet the criteria you have established. Taking the time to write down exactly how you will trade will force you to commit to the trade and see the market in that particular manner. Your trading ability will then keep improving because your virtues will demand that as your perceptions and abilities improve, your written plan of attack will also evolve.

When you sit down to write out your overall methodology, you will begin to internalize those rules and perceptions into your belief structure. This will require you to have faith that your beliefs about the market are valid. Without exception successful traders research, back-test, and then test in real time a new concept or belief before they include that particular belief in their written trading methodology. As you decide exactly how you will trade, you will have to determine the validity of a particular approach. In other words, if you read in a magazine that a particular indicator works with unbelievable success, then before your unconscious mind will accept its validity you will need to convince yourself of the validity of the author, the indicator, and the underlying beliefs that created the indicator.

There are five decisions that will either enhance or diminish your ability as a trader:

1. Your decision on what market behavior to focus on.
2. Your decision on what this behavior means to you.
3. Your decision about what to do to profit accordingly.
4. Your decision on what virtues to strengthen, and their related beliefs.
5. Your decision on what vices you will starve, and their related beliefs.

The vast majority of novice traders have never decided on anything other than that they want to trade, because they want to make huge profits. They have not taken the time to seriously contemplate the intellectual rigors demanded to trade.

To become a great trader, you must make sure that you learn from every trading experience. I know of no faster way to learn from your experiences than by making a real commitment on how you will trade. To maximize your ability to learn from each trading experience, you must make a commitment to write down in a trading journal every reason you entered a trade, moved a stop, and exited a trade. In addition to writing down your reasons, you must write down the emotions that you are experiencing while contemplating the trade. It is also helpful to write down how you physically are feeling. What you will discover is that your profitability is directly correlated to your methodology (naturally), emotional state, and physical state. Isn't that what controls your perception?

After recording your thoughts, reasons, physical well-being, and emotional state in a journal, you must review your log at least weekly. What you will realize is that the profits you earned, or the *losses you also earned,* are directly correlated to your overall well-being. It is virtually impossible to trade even a totally mechanical system if you are experiencing intense physical or emotional pain. In other words, even though you might have developed a trading methodology that is 100 percent mechanical, if you are in a state of intense pain, you will do something that will cause you to lose money, such as placing the order or the stop incorrectly.

So how do you develop your written trading methodology? Here are a series of questions that will get you on the correct path for getting long. Repeat questions 2 to 11 for getting short, and again for standing aside.

1. When you explain how the market works, what do you say?
    A. What metaphor would you use to explain the market to someone? Often a metaphor begins with "Trading is like...," "The market is like...," "When the market rises it is like...," "When trading it is like...."
2. How would you finish these sentences?
    A. "When the price goes up it is because..."
    B. "When the market stops going up it is because..."
    C. "I think the price is going up because..."
    D. "I think the price is about to go up because..."
    E. "When prices are going up, I begin thinking that the prices will falter when...."
3. What exactly must happen for you to go long?
4. What else should be happening for you to go long?
5. What should not be happening for you to go long?
6. What must not be happening for you to go long?
7. What are your exact money management rules?
8. Exactly how do you determine where your stop loss order is placed?
9. Exactly how do you determine that the market no longer possesses continuity of bullish thought?
    A. What exactly must happen for you to believe this?
    B. If the bulls are still in charge, what should be happening?
    C. What should not be happening if the bulls are in charge?
    D. What must the bulls not allow the bears to do if they are indeed still in charge?
10. Exactly how is your exit strategy determined?
11. Exactly how is your reentry strategy determined?

Your goal is to write down in the most clear and precise manner how you see the market, what must happen for you to get long or short, what has to happen to exit the trade, and what has to happen for you to stand aside. The more exactly you can describe your beliefs and rules, the more your ability as a trader will increase.

An important fact about the market that everyone knows, and yet the majority of traders conveniently forget, is that the market waits for no one. When you are trading, you are existing within a moment of time, and accordingly you must reach a decision within that moment of time. The moment of time that you exist in is a decision only you can make. When you are considering getting long, that is not the time to be wondering if your methodology is valid.

"A trader who hesitates has already lost."

When you commit your methodology to a piece of paper, you are creating a shortcut for your brain. All your brain has to do is to almost instantly take in all the relevant facts, and say "Yup, it all checks out—get long *now.*" Your brain will also let you know when your methodology is incorrect, or if it has become obsolete, assuming you have mastered your virtues, beliefs, and vices. Your ego will give you all the reasons that you do not need to take the time to commit your methodology to a piece of paper. This is because by writing down your methodology, you confront and dominate your ego in a manner that it is unable to escape from.

By writing down your beliefs, expectations, and rules, you will create certainty. Your level of confidence will increase dramatically, since you will no longer fear your own actions. Your level of discipline will increase, because you can no longer "fudge" your entry or exit. Since you took the time to research the validity of your trading methodology, and you have quantified all aspects of your methodology, the level of courage you have will also be vastly increased. Your mind no longer has to convince itself of the validity of the methodology employed, so it can allow some of the conscious mental energy to be diverted to the unconscious, thereby increasing your level of intuition. When you took the time to write your methodology down, you were also making a commitment to yourself that it was well worth the time to do so. This commitment dramatically increases the amount of time you will persist in the trading endeavor. Your integrity will increase so much that you will wonder why most traders don't write down their trading methodology!

20

FUNDAMENTAL ANALYSIS STRATEGIES

Fundamentals that you read about are typically useless as the market has already discounted the price, and I call them "funny-mentals." However, if you catch on early, before others believe, then you might have valuable "surprise-a-mentals."

—ED SEYKOTA

All my life I studied geography, politics, economics, and history intensely, believing they are interrelated, and I've used what I learned to invest in world markets.

—JIMMY ROGERS

Basically all of my trades are fundamentally oriented.

—JIMMY ROGERS

YOU ARE PROBABLY thinking "Just great, a series of quotes from famous traders that conflict with one another!" Well as you probably know by now, so what? Isn't flexibility a key requirement for success? Traders employ different methodologies. They all have similar convictions about the importance of empowering beliefs and virtues, how critical it is to control the vices of trading, and the importance of developing their own strategy. Whether you are a technical trader or a fundamental trader, you are still a trader concerned about making consistent profits.

In a previous chapter we talked about some of the technical tools that have served me very well over the years. When I first started trading stocks in the mid-1970s, I was a pure technical trader who didn't care one iota about the "funny-mentals." My belief at that time was that *all* known fundamental information was reflected in the price, in this instant of time. To a large degree I still believe that; however, there are times when the market gets so wound up in its own continuity of thought that nothing matters except that continuity of thought. There is a point, though, where the market gets so hysterical that it needs more "hysterical" traders. The instant the supply of new traders and/or new entry orders slows, the continuity of thought will collapse, along with the market.

Answer this question: Are you a technical trader or a fundamental trader? The majority of traders will answer that they are technical traders. The primary reason is that it takes less time to understand how a technical indicator works than to grasp the fundamentals. The human eye is very quick at picking up coincidences where the indicator did this, and the market did that. Consequently most traders buy a computer and get a trading program with all the technical indicators built in, and low and behold within a relatively short period of time they are "expert market technicians"!

Becoming an expert on how fundamentals and intermarket relationships might affect price requires an intense amount of study. Heck, there are people who go to college for years to understand the big picture! It is one thing to write a program to perform a mathematical operation on the price, but it is another thing to write a program to include all the different variables that constitute the fundamentals. Whereas the most popular technical indicators are visually appealing and require little thought (to a novice), fundamentals are not visually appealing and require a lot of thought. Much like a GO game.

As I have stressed, there is no right or wrong answer in devising a trading methodology. However, it behooves you to understand some of the rudimentary aspects of the markets you are trading. Every single market is ruled by internal relationships, to some degree or another. What is the underlying reason that a market will enter into a multiyear bear phase? Why has gold, for example, slowly drifted down for the past decade? What is the underlying reason that markets trend? The underlying reason is that supply and demand are not balanced. One force is more powerful than the other, and consequently the price will trend.

Why does a market trend up? For several reasons: The supply decreased and the demand increased. The demand decreased slower than the supply decreased. The supply increased, but the demand increased faster. The supply remained fixed, and the demand increased.

Why does a market trend down? For the exact opposite reasons it trends up. Why does a market go sideways? Because the supply meets the demand so that it is perfectly balanced. What does the price represent? In all cases the price represents the level where demand meets supply, and becomes a number. As a trader, your responsibility is to use every tool and piece of information available to profit from the movement of prices. Technical analysis gives a trader valuable information, fundamentals give a trader valuable news. It is critical to understand that both demand the profitable trader to *think!*

Often different markets are interrelated. This is easily observed while simultaneously looking at different charts. For example, recently there has been a correlation between the Japanese yen and the price of crude oil. In a purely technical sense this correlation is easily understood. That is, if yen goes up, then crude is going to rally. However, the trader who actually understands the fundamental reasons this is taking place is in a position to catch the break in the continuity of thought, possibly before a pure technical trader. When you are trading a market, every bit of understanding that you can apply to that market will help give you an edge.

Is it harder to create a methodology that incorporates fundamentals? Of course! Do novice traders thoroughly understand both? Of course not, because that would take too much work! The amount of knowledge you can bring to bear on any market will be partially dependent upon the extent that you can incorporate fundamentals into your methodology. As you gain experience, your level of general knowledge will also increase, allowing you to incorporate more knowledge into your methodology.

When a market begins to move in a particular direction, it does so for a technical and/or fundamental reason. Paradoxically when a market has a valid fundamental reason to change direction, it will often initially ignore that fundamental. In other words, if there is a rip-roaring bull market, technical analysis will tell you that the market is in a solid up trend. However, the fundamentals could be telling you that these high prices are not the reflection of solid demand from real users of the commodity; instead, speculators are buying the commodity only because the price went up in the past. Thus the market is being propelled higher out of a basic human vice, greed. Unless something happens to change the demand/supply equation, the constantly increasing prices are eventually doomed. What eventually happens is that the continuity of thought is broken, and the prices then plummet. What event fundamentally or technically do you think could cause this break in the continuity of thought?

So do you go short when you realize that the market is demonstrating a high degree of hysteria? You can go short only when your methodology tells you to get short. Now if your methodology incorporates a "hysteria" factor within it, and it is indicating that you should get short, then you would get short. However, I would urge you to realize that often this could lead to substantial losses, since it is very difficult to pick a point right before the crowd stops buying hysterically. It might be more advantageous to wait for the high and to go short after the hysteria, and its related continuity of thought, has broken. Another possibility is to wait for the market to hit a high and collapse, and then attempt to retest the high getting short at that point. Again there is no correct way; you have to create your own technique.

Perhaps a plan to trade using fundamentals and technicals would be to go long as soon as the technical gave a buy signal, and increase the position size as the fundamentals confirm the bullish continuity of thought. Then, as the fundamentals or the technicals (whichever come first) start indicating weakness, lighten the position size and, when one of them turns bearish, go flat.

The more you can understand about a market that you trade in, the more you improve the possibility of making a profit. Does this mean that you must become an expert? Depends on you, and how your methodology evolves. I suspect that the more you know about the commodity, the more you will enjoy trading it. The more you understand fundamentally about how certain events affect the commodity you are trading, the larger your "edge" becomes.

This extra knowledge takes on considerable importance at market turns. Many times when the market is beginning to turn, your methodology—if it is strictly based upon technical factors—will get you into trades that subsequently fail, resulting in a loss. Now if, while you were creating your methodology, you included a component consisting of fundamental factors, then as the market begins to change the subsequent technical signals will be counterbalanced by the fundamental components of the methodology. By ignoring these subsequent signals, you prevent yourself from being stopped out repeatedly. The trick here is that the fundamental picture will change a little differently each time.

I urge you to learn as much as you possibly can about all the inter- and intramarket relationships in every market you trade in. For example, if you are trading soybean oil, do you know how coconut oil might affect soybean oil prices? If not, perhaps you might want to read up on that interrelationship. Perhaps your trading methodology will not even consider fundamentals; that is fine. After all, your methodology represents your unique perspective on the market. Even if your methodology has no fundamental component, I urge you to become aware of the key fundamentals about the contracts you are trading in. If for no other reason, the additional knowledge will help you enjoy trading a little bit more.

In Appendix B you will find a list of Internet sites that you can visit to help increase your level of fundamental knowledge. As I look at a wide variety of markets, I enjoy visiting a variety of Web sites to get news. A trick that I have found is to read the Internet version of foreign newspapers. This helps me realize on a daily basis that even though the United States is a vital part of the overall global economy, there are other perspectives that carry a lot of validity. These foreign perspectives are quite naturally affected by the developments within their countries, and worldwide. Consequently the price movement of a market that I am trading in, or a related market, will be affected by international factors. How was this knowledge beneficial? Let me give you an example. In 1997 the Malaysian currency devalued, and this affected the value of the currencies of nearby countries. The devaluation dramatically increased the cost of Malaysian imports and lowered the cost of exports. Two commodities I was trading that were affected were crude oil and soybeans.

Without going into all the reasons why, it became very apparent to me that the price of crude would have to drop, and the price of soybean oil would also have to drop. Consequently I waited for these two commodities to give me a sell signal using my methodology. The ability to wait for the sell signal depends on how strong your virtues are. My success was that the fundamentals gave me a clear signal on decreasing demand with the supply not being affected, indicating lower prices. My primary technical methodology then gave me my exact entry point.

The more you learn about fundamentals, the more profitable you will become. Understanding the "big" picture will also give you the confidence to stay with a trending market longer.

21

COMPUTER SYSTEMS AND THE FALLACY OF OPTIMIZATION

Over time I have become more mechanical, since (1) I have become more trusting of trend trading, and (2) my mechanical programs have factored in more and more "tricks of the trade." I still go through periods of thinking that I can out-perform my own system, but such excursions are often self-correcting through the process of losing money.

—ED SEYKOTA

The point is that because people are the same, if you use sufficiently rigorous method to avoid hindsight, you can test a system and see how it would have done in the past and get a fairly good idea of how that system will perform in the future. That is our edge.

—LARRY HITE

COMPUTERS ARE AMONG the most common pieces of equipment that traders use. Unfortunately, the vast majority of traders are engaging their computer to enter into trades, without engaging their mind to think! There is a huge difference between buying a computer trading system and sitting down to do the research to develop your own computer-based trading system. Any computer-based trading system that you buy might be profitable (in sales or trading) to its author; however, to a trader that is not intimately familiar with the research behind it, and why the rules exist, the program is basically worthless.

The vast majority of successful traders developed a methodology by building their own trading system from the ground up. As they devise their trading strategy, they very well could have used indicators, beliefs, and subsystem rules by purchasing them, studying them, or learning them from a more experienced trader. The distinction is that until the techniques have been verified, studied, and invariably modified, the trader will not use them. Only after constant experimentation with the new idea, and after verifying and internalizing, and then deciding that the idea is valid and valuable, does the trader add the new concept to his or her methodology.

What steps do you think has to happen for traders to develop a personal trading methodology?

1. Traders must first determine how they will perceive the way the market operates. They need to develop a metaphor and beliefs that accurately describe the market action *in their minds*.

2. They must then have the beliefs that allow them to perceive consistently recurring market events.

3. These events must be consistent, identifiable, and quantifiable. They must be instantly identifiable in the future.

4. Traders must test these events to determine their validity and probability of repeating.

5. After all the research, validating, and probability studies are done, traders will sit down and write out their methodology. They will make a commitment to a methodology—to always trade by its rules.

6. Traders (or their programmers) will sit down at a computer and attempt to write a trading program that incorporates as much of this trading methodology as possible.

7. When the program is done, traders are able to tell quickly what action they must take. The important point to realize is that the traders are now intimately familiar with all the related studies.

As you come up with your own trading methodology, you should refer back to these steps. Unfortunately, designing a computer trading system that accurately reflects your trading methodology demands a lot of time. It is not something that you can put together over a weekend. However, the huge advantage is that when you are done, you have accomplished something that 98 percent of all traders never do. Consequently you will see your trades produce consistent results. Once you are producing consistent results, *either profitable or not,* you can begin working on your ability to perceive the market better. As your perception increases, your ability to produce consistent profits will increase. It should be stressed that in order to have the internal beliefs required to do the research necessary to develop your methodology, you must make a decision to become responsible for *all* your beliefs.

At some point all traders must confront how they will use the power of the computer to optimize their trading methodology. For those traders who are unfamiliar with optimization, allow me to briefly describe it. Optimization is achieved when you have written a mathematical formula or theory that describes the market action (in part or wholly) through variables. By programming the computer to literally perform all the mathematical permutations possible on the variables, and then correlating these permutations to the profitability, you can determine the variables that created the most profit. In other words, by determining the best combination of variables to maximize profitability, you can create a highly profitable methodology. The only problem is that it is good only for historical data; *it is absolutely worthless in real time.*

Say we have a simple moving-average crossover trading system. Our rules are very simple. First, if the short-period moving average goes above the longer-term moving average, go long. Second, if the shorter moving average goes under the longer moving average, go short. Consequently we are always long or short. By writing (or buying) a program, we can specify that we want to vary the shorter moving average from a period of 2 to 20, and the longer period from 21 to 60. Then by allowing the computer to test all the permutations that could occur by varying the periods of the shorter and the longer moving average, and by keeping track of the profitability, we can determine the most profitable short-term and long-term moving average. For example, the computer might indicate that a shorter moving average of 15 days and a longer-term moving average of 57 days generates the best profit. Typically the second most profitable combination of variables will generate less than half as much profits as the most profitable combination!

At this point most beginning traders are very excited, convinced that they have just found the holy grail! There is a huge problem here. These traders have just wasted some very valuable time programming, because all they have accomplished is to curve-fit their variables to historical data. While it appears to be an outstanding combination of variables, it is an outstanding combination because it is *only* looking at the specific data used to perform the permutations. In other words, if they modified the data by changing either the dates used or the contracts, and reperformed the computer optimization study, they would come up with different short-term and long-term moving average values.

All traders use optimization studies to one degree or another. It is important to realize that by varying the length of the data used and by using different contracts, the value of your variables will vary. If you do in fact optimize your indicators and trading system, your goal is to find a group of variables that perform equally well on different contracts and different time periods.

When you start analyzing the profitability of the various variables, you should automatically discard the *variables* that generated profits far in excess of any other profitable variables. Why? Suppose that a certain set of variables generated profits of $2000 and the second most profitable set of variables generated profits of $1000, and the third most profitable set of variables generated the profits of $950. Then it would be safe to say that the variables that generated the profits of $2000 are so optimized that they are worthless.

Your goal whenever you are doing optimization studies is to come up with a set of variables that perform equally well on different commodities, using a wide variety of different data lengths and, perhaps most important, using commodities that are clearly in bull and bear markets. The last point requires a little expansion. Lately there have been some very good computer-based systems that have generated profits. Typically, however, the system is geared only toward a bull market. When the market goes sideways or actually drops, the system loses a lot of money. It is important as you devise your system to look at the widest possible variety of markets, trends, and time frames.

When you are developing your methodology, keep in mind that you will be trading in markets dominated by bulls, markets dominated by bears, and markets where everyone is snoozing. You want your trading methodology to reflect this fact. An outstanding methodology will be profitable in all markets, in all time frames, and across all trends.

In order to design your computer-based trading methodology (if indeed you decide to use one), you must make a commitment to the time and intellectual power that will be required. Naturally enough, you will need to strengthen the beliefs that empower you, constantly improve your virtues, and annihilate your vices.

22

LENGTH OF TIME TO MASTER TRADING SKILLS

Don't speculate unless you can make it a full time job.

—BERNARD BARUCH

A LL TOO OFTEN people starting out in a new endeavor have an urge to run before they can walk. Typically their ego is in the driver's seat and wants the satisfaction of immediate action. However, it is a realistic question to ask: How long before a level of competency is established? Unfortunately, the answer can only be somewhat vague, since it really depends on how committed the individual is. This level of commitment will dictate how much energy is placed into mastering the required skills.

In order to become an outstanding trader, you will need a large number of references, a valid belief structure, and the ability to "internalize" your new skills, perceptions, and beliefs. The more references you experience, the more refined your distinctions can be. The references can come from other individuals.

There are several seminars that I highly recommend. My favorite is "Date with Destiny," offered by Anthony Robbins. "Date with Destiny" is intended to help you clarify your goals, beliefs, values, and rules. Although it is not specifically designed for traders, I know many who have attended with great benefit. Another good resource is Dr. Richard McCall, a practicing psychologist who is also a shishan of the Bushinkai Dojo, where he teaches the traditional martial disciplines and the philosophies of the Japanese samurai, including Budo-Zen. Dr. McCall offers several retreats that also work with the mental beliefs a trader must have. Since these seminars are geared toward traders, the information is invaluable. Finally, there are a variety of technical analysis seminars available. My favorite is the TAG conference held in Las Vegas, usually in October or November.

Books and audiotapes are also a valuable way to obtain more distinctions. A new and useful source of information are the various e-mail lists that you can subscribe to. For example, since I use Omega Trade Station (version 4), I subscribe to the Omega e-mail list. While the vast majority of the information on the list is geared to technical problems that users are experiencing, occasionally there will be a posting (1 in 300) that is informative. The main thing to keep in the back of your mind is that the traders who produce consistent profits are too busy trading to send e-mail, while the novices have a lot of time to post comments. The best posts seem to occur over the weekends, which is not surprising. A sampling of all these resources is presented in Appendix B.

The most valuable references that you can obtain are quite naturally those that you actually experience. Every time you encounter a new event, your mind is using it to either create a new belief or reinforce an old belief. By applying the techniques in this book, you will be able to challenge your "old" perception of events. Consequently you will begin to adopt new beliefs that will increase your ability to perceive the markets. As you trade real money, you will have to constantly reinforce your empowering beliefs. By using sensible risk control parameters, you will financially survive long enough to make better and better distinctions.

The ability to execute a trade free of errors is a skill that is mastered through repetition. Your desire should be to execute the placement of your order with a procedure that eliminates the possibility of error. As you consistently apply your new beliefs while experiencing new events, your ability will steadily increase.

The time it takes you to become a consistently profitable trader will also depend upon your ability to clearly define what your beliefs are. What is the market? Is it a friend or a foe? Is it fun to trade or a struggle? What is a bear/bull trend? What is a loss? What is profit? What are your beliefs about your own identity? What are your goals regarding trading? Have you mastered your virtues? Have you controlled your vices? What do you believe about learning? Is learning fun? Can you have a flexible mind? Do you believe that you have the ability to perceive the beliefs of others? Can you perceive why others are behaving the way they are? What are your beliefs about the length of time it takes to actually learn and use new information? What are your beliefs about awareness? What are your beliefs about accepting the behavior of the market, others, or yourself?

The length of time it takes you to master trading is totally dependent upon how long it takes to master yourself. People who excel in any activity are excellent because they have *become* their new beliefs and distinctions. *They are not trying to be confident; they are confident. They are not trying to trade free of fear; they have no fear.* The act of trying means that you are still not there. *Trying* to accomplish anything will only guarantee you more frustration.

It is easy to know intellectually what needs to be done. It is an entirely different matter to do it. The very first step that you must take is a "leap of faith." Once you have the faith that you will become all that you desire, then you will become what you desire. As always, the first step is the most difficult.

Shortly after I went to "Date with Destiny" by Anthony Robbins and a retreat by Dr. Richard McCall, a little light went on inside my brain. Finally I understood: The secret that all traders are looking for is not in some indicator, system, or computer program. Rather, the secret to becoming a successful trader lies in mastering the ability to think and enhance certain internal values, beliefs, and rules. In other words, the virtues that an individual consistently uses on a daily basis are the largest single factor in his or her eventual success. The seminars were worth several times what I paid, since I learned not only how to lead a much happier life, but also what the secret of trading really was.

All consistently successful traders get to a point where the market lives inside them. No longer are they looking at the market from an outside perspective; rather, they are "one" with the market. Most traders who stay in this business for more than a few years have realized that the market will never validate their beliefs or actions. They know that the market is nothing more than a reflection of their own internal beliefs and representations. In order to become consistently profitable traders, they had to change their beliefs to accommodate the market.

By adopting the same beliefs and rules that more successful individuals use, you can greatly reduce the amount of time required to master *any* subject. A great deal of research will still need to be done, and of course there is still a fairly steep learning curve. However, the amount of time required can easily be cut in half.

While this chapter is short, I trust that you have come to the realization that successful trading is within your grasp. All you have to do is be willing to expand the repertoire of skills that you need to trade. You must make a commitment to excel at an admittedly difficult endeavor. The amount of time to master trading may be dramatically shortened; however, a certain amount of "dues" will still have to be paid.

BRINGING IT ALL TOGETHER

There is nothing training cannot do. Nothing is above its reach. It can turn bad morals to good; it can destroy bad principles and recreate good ones; it can lift men to angelship.

—MARK TWAIN

It's more important to want to make money than to want to be "right." People who want to be right all the time are afraid to make decisions. People who want to make money are willing to change their decisions to take what the market will give them.

—TOM R. PETERSON

EFFECTIVE TRAINING BASED upon valid beliefs will allow you the freedom to accomplish the goals that you desire. While training, you will begin to increase your virtues, diminish your vices, and transform yourself into the trader you desire to be. The one thing that everyone has absolute control over is deciding what virtues must be acquired, and what vices must be eliminated. Every day you decide how you will live your life. The daily decisions that you make are a reflection of what beliefs and virtues you hold dear to your heart, and what vices you will tolerate.

Your trading account is a very accurate indication of your abilities as a trader. Your abilities as a trader will derive from the ability of your trading methodology to function over time, in all trading environments. The ability of your trading methodology to consistently generate profitable trades will be a result of possessing the required beliefs to develop your own trading methodology.

The really great thing about trading is that the financial rewards, though immense, are dwarfed by the gigantic rewards to the trader's beliefs and character traits. The difficulty of trading is the very thing that makes it great. Often when people are surrounded by seemingly incredible difficulties, that is the exact time their virtues and beliefs are increased (assuming they want to rise above the challenge). It is human nature to do everything possible to avoid incredible difficulties. However, when novices decide to trade, seemingly insurmountable difficulties will always lie just around the next curve. The question is: When they realize that trading is far more difficult than they had initially thought, will they give up?

It is very easy to give into the vices that trading generates. Egotism, uncertainty, envy, contempt, anxiety, fear, frustration, anger, lying, confusion, lack of persistence, resentment, and doubt are just some of the vices. It is very easy for novice traders to accept that their current beliefs about what it takes to make money while trading are valid, even while they are losing money. It is also very easy for novice traders to transfer their responsibility for making money to others. A vice is always easy to embrace and live with! Likewise, a virtue is initially difficult to embrace and to practice!

Wealth will always flow to those who have the correct beliefs about wealth, just as water will always seek its own level. A really great thing about trading is that the market will always tell you the validity of your beliefs and virtues. Traders with really poor beliefs about themselves and the market, with a correspondingly small number of virtues, will be rewarded by the marketplace with small profits (if any). Veteran traders know that when measured over time, their profitability will be a reflection of the quality of their beliefs and virtues.

My goal in writing this book has been to state the cold, hard truths of trading. While I was at Lind-Waldock, the fundamental truth of trading was irrefutable. It is unavoidable to notice the irrefutable truths of trading when you talk to hundreds of different traders each month. Far fewer books discuss the psychological aspects of trading than discuss some technical aspect of the market. The vast majority of books focus on an "external" technical methodology. Far fewer adequately address the far more important "internal" character traits that successful trading demands. If you get nothing else from this book, get this: *If the great majority of individuals are doing what you anticipate doing, and they are getting results that you want to avoid, then by God do not do what they did!*

Every chapter of this book is designed to get you to understand the key beliefs all successful traders depend upon. Everything discussed is under your direct control, for you to gain mastery of. All it takes is a willingness on your part to decide to accept responsibility for your trading performance. The most important concept to understand is that it is your existing beliefs that have brought you to where you are now. If where you want to go is someplace different, then you must come up with the beliefs that will let you accomplish that goal. Before you can come up with these new beliefs, you will have to make a *decision*. You must decide to discard or modify old beliefs and obtain some new, enabling beliefs.

In order for you to take that step, you must first clarify what your present beliefs are. When you know what beliefs you are currently using, you will be able to determine if they are helping or preventing you from becoming a better trader. You will have to decide if they are based upon a virtue or a vice. All great traders have a solid grasp of their values and beliefs. They walk their talk, because they have a deep inner power. People have power when they congruently live by their virtues and beliefs. The power of successful traders to consistently earn profits is based on their ability to consistently increase their virtues and diminish their vices.

For many of these successful traders, a significant event that created immense emotional stress forced them to decide exactly what beliefs and virtues they were going to live and die by. When they made the decision on what their new beliefs would be, they also made a decision to consistently apply them. This decision meant that no matter what, even if it brought them pain, they would not waver in applying their new beliefs.

Most successful traders realize that it is not the price movement of the market that is controlling their profitability but the way they perceive and interpret that price movement. Their perceptions are controlled by their beliefs about the market, which in turn are controlled by the strength of their values and vices.

As you start developing your overall methodology, always strive to ask yourself the highest-quality questions that you can think of. The better the quality of your questions, the better the quality of your methodology. The reason that successful traders became successful is that they constantly asked themselves questions on how they could better exercise their virtues, create empowering beliefs, and devise a better trading methodology. Consequently they were constantly improving their methodology, beliefs, and virtues. By consistently asking effective questions, they were able to control their focus. Your unconscious and conscious mind will bend over backward to achieve what you are focusing on.

Questions have an unbelievable power on your ultimate success. Too often novice traders consistently ask questions that focus attention on their vices. For example, after losing money, many traders will ask themselves a lousy question such as this: "Why didn't I realize the trend was down before I went long?" This is a very negative question, since the answer will only focus their attention on a vice such as fear, not accepting responsibility, and doubt. A much better question is: "What can I learn from this experience?" Here the focus is on the virtues, such as confidence and certainty, and in order to create more certainty, more research must be done. In addition to the quality of the questions is their sheer number. Ask as many questions as you can think of: *Successful traders become successful because they ask questions that the novice traders fail to ask.*

By asking questions, you can change your focus, and therefore what you are feeling. Empowering questions after losing money include: "What's great about this?" "What can I learn from this?" A negative question is: "How come I can never make any money?" As you develop your methodology and start working on increasing your virtues, your brain is prioritizing what to pay attention to. However, since the amount of information the market presents is huge and comes at you so fast, your conscious brain is rather limited on how many different pieces of information it can concentrate on. Consequently your brain is very busy prioritizing what not to pay attention to.

In order to be angry, a trader must not be paying attention to all the reasons for feeling happy. In other words, if the last trade resulted in a major loss, the trader will be paying attention to a lot of thoughts related to that loss. Consequently the trader will not be paying attention to reasons for feeling happy. The trader is focusing only on certain thoughts and ignoring others.

Now if our trader would decide to ask an enabling question like "What could I learn from this trade, so that this loss never happens again?" then the trader will begin focusing on an entirely different set of thoughts, and will no longer be as angry. Excellent traders consistently ask themselves questions that enable them to strengthen their virtues and to create a profitable trading methodology.

We have come full circle. Your success as a trader will be determined by the quality of your decisions. You will have to decide if you think there is any validity to what I have had to say. I suspect that you will be able to recognize the truth—even if it is something you don't want to hear. Trading is the most difficult profession there is, and once mastered it is also the easiest way to make money. Trading has the potential to create immense intellectual rewards, as well as the potential for immense psychological pain.

Every individual on this planet is on a journey toward individual (consciously or unconsciously) chosen goals. Those individuals who are able to control their mind by possessing faith that their virtues will triumph are the ones who succeed massively. Trading allows them to master fear, anxiety, anger, and resentment by exercising confidence, discipline, courage, intuition, and persistence. As their virtues continue to gain in strength, and their vices continue to weaken, they arrive at their goal of trading from a position of total integrity.

COMPARISON TABLE OF VIRTUES VERSUS VICES

Faith	attacks	Doubt
Confidence	attacks	Fear
Discipline	attacks	Indecision
Courage	attacks	Anger
Intuition	builds	Insight
Persistence	builds	Accomplishments
Flexibility	builds	Growth
Integrity	demands	Virtues

RESOURCES

INTERNET

News List Servers

misc.invest.futures
misc.invest.stocks
misc.invest.technical

E-Mail List

Omega List is an independent e-mail list that discusses technical
difficulties and trading challenges. Send an e-mail to
omega-list-request@eskimo.com.

Edward Toppel has an e-mail digest that he sends out. To subscribe,
visit his Web site at http://www.samuraitrader.com.

Real Traders is an independent e-mail list sponsored by Kasanjian
Research that discusses technical and some fundamental aspects
of trading. Send an c-mail to support@realtraders.com or
call 909-337-0816.

John Hayden may be contacted at jhayden@today.com.au or you
can visit his Web site at http://www.sente.net. To be notified of
new articles and books by John Hayden, send an e-mail to
notify@sente.net. His business e-mail address is
JHayden@DirectionalResearch.com, and his business Web site
is http://www.directionalresearch.com.

WEB SITES

Commodities

http://www.cardwellfg.com	Andrew Cardwell CTA
http://www.adtrading.com	Applied Derivatives Trading Magazine
http://www.thectr.com	Center for Futures Education, Inc.
http://exchanges.quotewatch.com	Delayed Quote on Different Exchanges
http://www.weather.net	Freese-Notis Weather
http://www.murphymorris.com	John Murphy

Stocks

http://www.wallstreetcity.com   An excellent source of information for
stock traders. Their delayed intraday charts are perhaps the best.
http://www.thestreet.com   Another excellent source of information for stock traders.

Exchanges

http://www.amex.com	American Stock Exchange
http://www.financeweb.ase.nl	Amsterdam Exchange
http://www.cbot.com	Chicago Board of Trade
http://www.cboe.com	Chicago Board Options Exchange (CBOE)
http://www.cme.com	Chicago Mercantile Exchange

http://www.gni.co.uk	GNI Limited
http://www.hkfe.com	Hong Kong Futures Exchange
http://www.liffe.com	London International Financial Futures Exchange (LIFFE)
http://www.lme.co.uk	London Metal Exchange
http://www.csce.com	New York Coffee, Sugar, and Cocoa Exchange
http://www.nymex.com	New York Mercantile Exchange
http://www.nyce.com	New York Cotton Exchange
http://www.kcbt.com	Kansas City Board of Trade
http://www.kse.or.kr	Korea Stock Exchange
http://www.matif.fr	Marche à Terme Internationale de France (MATIF SA)
http://www.meff.es	MEFF Renta Fija
http://www.midam.com	Mid America Commodity Exchange
http://www.mgex.com	Minneapolis Grain Exchange
http://www.me.org	Montreal Exchange
http://www.nymex.com	New York Mercantile Exchange
http://www.nyse.com	New York Stock Exchange
http://www.ose.or.jp/index_e.htm	Osaka Securities Exchange
http://www.simex.com.sg	Singapore International Monetary Exchange (SIMEX)
http://www.sfe.com.au	Sydney Futures Exchange
http://www.tge.or.jp	Tokyo Grain Exchange
http://www.tiffe.or.jp	Tokyo International
http://www.wce.mb.ca	Winnipeg Commodity Exchange

SEMINARS

Robbins Research Institute
9191 Towne Centre Drive, Suite 600
San Diego, CA 92122
http://anthonyrobbins.com
800-898-8669
Contact: Kevin Teeple, Ext. 6345

Dr. Richard McCall
P.O. Box 23413
Little Rock, AR 72221
800-336-7061

SOFTWARE

Software for plotting prices and the various formulas is made by:

Stratagem Software
800-779-7353
http://members.aol.com/stratagem1

Index

About the Author

John Hayden is a full-time trader and the director of risk management at Directional Research and Trading, Inc., an offshore hedge fund based in New York. He has successfully traded the stock, cash, and futures markets for over 20 years. A former account manager for managed money at Lind-Waldock and commodities analysis partner to CTA Andrew Cardwell, Hayden speaks extensively to working brokers and brokerage houses.